Theodore W. Whitley, Ph.D.
East Carolina University, Greenville

STUDY GUIDE
for

PSYCHOLOGY

SIXTH EDITION

Stephen F. Davis
Morningside College

Joseph J. Palladino
University of Southern Indiana

PEARSON

Prentice
Hall

Upper Saddle River, New Jersey 07458

© 2010 by PEARSON EDUCATION, INC.
Upper Saddle River, New Jersey 07458

10 9 8 7 6 5 4 3 2 1

ISBN 10: 0-205-67179-9
ISBN 13: 978-0-205-67179-3

Contents

How to Use the Study Guide

This manual was created especially for you. The format of the manual conforms exactly to the textbook, *Psychology,* Sixth Edition, by Drs. Stephen Davis and Joseph Palladino. Use this manual when you study the textbook and when you prepare for tests. Each chapter of the study guide contains an outline taken exactly from the corresponding chapter in the textbook. To get the most from each resource, and from your psychology class, find a place to study where you can see all your material for the course at one time. Each chapter included the following sections.

Outline. Each study guide chapter includes an outline of the corresponding textbook chapter in the textbook with space for taking notes or writing questions that occur to you as you study the text. The outline includes references to the *Psychological Detective, Hands On, Myth or Science,* and *Study Tip* activities as they occur in the textbook. The following icons identify these sections.

Psychological Detective

Hands On

Myth or Science

Study Tip

Chapter Practice Tests. Each chapter includes multiple-choice items, completion items, and critical thinking exercises that you should attempt after you have studied the material in the relevant chapter. The critical thinking exercises are included as part of the practice tests to help you apply concepts that you have learned in each chapter. Correct responses and explanations are presented at the end of the section.

Key Vocabulary Terms. Key terms from the chapter, presented in the order in which they appear in the textbook, are listed at the end of each chapter.

Good Luck! I hope you find your introductory psychology course to be both challenging and informative. The concepts that you will learn in this course will be valuable to you in years to come.

Tip for Success: Getting the Most from Your Textbook

Textbooks are densely packed with information and can be exhausting to read. Studying your textbook must be an *active* process in order for you to gain the most from it. It is unfortunate that perhaps the most widely used method for studying a textbook is probably the least effective. Look around at your classmates' books and notice how many people highlight or underline passages of text with fluorescent markers. *Indiscriminate* highlighting is a common practice among students who are at the early stages of learning to study. If you prefer to highlight, fine. The important thing is to consider carefully the text you will highlight, and why you are highlighting it.

Material should be highlighted because you plan to reread the passage later. If each page looks as if it has been dipped in a bucket of ink, the notion of rereading highlighted material can be daunting. As a result, many students never reread the material they took so much time highlighting.

It is better to study a chapter over several study sessions rather than in a single sitting. Consider the *serial position effect* (see Chapter 7, Memory). According to the serial position effect, you will remember the most from the first and last portions of your study sessions. With this in mind, there are two things to consider when organizing your study sessions: 1) *minimize the middle* portion of your study sessions, and 2) *study actively.*

By creating several study sessions, you will be minimizing the middle portion, or extending the "ends" of your study session. You will take advantage of the primacy (early part of study session) and recency (last part of study session) components of the serial position effect. By making the process of studying active, you will capitalize on what you will learn about levels of processing in the chapter on memory. In brief, the deeper you process information, the greater your chances of remembering the information.

In addition to using this study guide, two well-known approaches may help you study your textbook more efficiently and effectively. Try different approaches until you find a good fit for your learning style.

What Does Work

Methods for studying textbook material have been developed over the years. A combination of these methods may be the best approach. In addition to considering the merits of the following methods, know that this study guide was organized expressly for facilitating the process of extracting information from your textbook. First, the two main methods for studying text:

1. SQ3R. This acronym that stands for steps in the process of studying text: Survey, Question, Read, Recall, and Review.
  a. Survey. Spend several minutes orienting yourself to the material you are about to study. Knowing where you are headed will make it far easier to recognize the key landmarks along the way. The following sub-steps should be part of the survey step: examine chapter overviews, read summaries at the end of chapters, and read the headings throughout the chapter. Take time to look at the figures and tables and note how they fit with the sections of the text with which they are associated.
  b. Question. As you begin studying either a single paragraph or a larger portion of a chapter, first stop and ask yourself what you are about to learn. Write things down. This can be as simple as rephrasing a paragraph heading into a question. Do not rely on your memory. Write it down.
  c. Read. Having surveyed the material and prepared yourself by asking what you expect to learn, you will be prepared to read. Read with the questions you posed in mind. Do not get bogged down and spend your time staring at words. If you cannot remember what you just read, you are not reading effectively. One way to keep from bogging down is to keep track of how much time you spend reading each page. If you push yourself slightly, you will retain more than if you slow down and relax too much while you read. Summarize the main points from what you read in your notebook, making sure the summary is in your own words. By translating the messages from the text into *your own language,* you are processing it, and thereby improving your chances of remembering it.
  d. Recite. Look away from your book and notes, even close your eyes if it helps, and use mental imagery to recall what you just read. What words stand out? What information was communicated in the tables and figures? If you were to draw a diagram or picture to represent the information, what would it look like?

e. Review. Refer to your questions, notes from reading, and textbook questions to see how well you recalled the information. Note any omissions. What material needs more attention? Do not proceed until you master each page. Benefitting from subsequent paragraphs and pages is difficult if you do not understand the ones you have already read.

This method may sound like a time-consuming way to read; however, in the end, it is efficient. Take time to learn the material during your first exposure, and you will save having to reread later. If you plan a study session with the idea of finishing a portion of a chapter, rather than trying to study the entire chapter in a single sitting, you will find that you can make better use of discrete chunks of time.

Many students use the next technique, the *Notes in the Margin Method,* effectively by itself. However, consider using it in conjunction with the SQ3R method to improve your potential for learning the material.

2. Notes in the Margin Method. Quite literally, this technique involves using the blank space in your textbook to record notes as you read. However, you may wish to record your notes in a notebook to preserve the quality of your book and to reduce the risk of overlooking some of your comments as you review.

> **a. Do Not Highlight Your Text as You Read.** Having identified a reason to read a paragraph (see B, above, for comments on asking questions), you are ready to read. Read with an eye for information that will be mentioned in class lectures and discussions, or will appear on tests.
>
> **b. Adopt Your Professor's Perspective.** After reading a section of text, adopt your professor's perspective to write a question or two in your notebook. If you develop your skills at *asking questions,* including multiple choice items with all the alternatives, you will also develop your skills for *answering questions.*
>
> **c. Refer to the Text.** Next, find the passage in the text that provides the answer to your question. This is the material you could underline or highlight. Better yet, translate the passage into your own words and write it in your notes.
>
> **d. Study Your Notes.** If your goal is to learn course content, study your notes from the textbook and test yourself with your own questions. Active note taking will help you learn; and studying your notes adds to the effect.

3. Using this Study Guide. The chapters in this study guide were organized to help you obtain maximum benefit from your textbook. Pay attention to the structure of the outline and the diagrams. Which sections are related to larger topics from the text? How are the key vocabulary terms related to the material you are studying? The following suggestions may help you combine the methods described above and make the best use of this study guide.

> **a. Examine the Outline in this Study Guide.** Each outline in this study guide, which always follows the chapter overview, was taken directly from the textbook. When surveying the material you are about to study, you may find it helpful to study the outline from the study guide first.
>
> **b. Learn the Language.** Many students struggle with the language of psychology. Each chapter of the study guide includes a list of key terms from the chapter. The key words are listed at the end of the study guide chapters and are presented in the order in which they are presented in the textbook. Take time to record a definition for each word. Do this *in your own words,* rather than copying verbatim from the textbook. Be sure to study the terms printed in italics in the text, especially those mentioned by your instructor in lectures.
>
> **c. Use the Space.** In addition to providing space for rewriting key word definitions, you will find space to make a few summarizing comments for each section of each chapter. Use this space.
>
> **d. Work through the Study Guide!** Be sure to complete the chapter outlines and take the chapter tests.

You will have noticed that each of the suggestions for using your textbook involved *active* processing of the material. If you do not study the material actively, chances are you will not gain as much from your efforts. Also, make sure to study only for reasonable units of time. If you can *minimize the middle* portions of your study sessions, you will retain the most from them.

Tips for Success: Preparing For and Taking Tests

The tests you will take in your psychology course will probably include some multiple-choice items, and all the items may be presented in this format. The primary purpose of this study guide is to help you excel in the course by retaining and understanding the information presented in the textbook and by performing well on the tests. In the best circumstances, tests are instruments that serve both professors and students. Professors rely on them for measuring student progress, and students use them for feedback on the depth and breadth of their understanding. Additionally, students can use tests to demonstrate their enthusiasm for a course. For many students, taking tests is the only way they communicate with their instructors.

Because tests are usually linked to course grades, it is common for students to become anxious about them. Unfortunately, anxiety sometimes distracts students from focusing entirely on content when preparing for tests, and from performing their best when taking tests. This section was developed as a guide to preparing for and taking tests, and hopefully will reduce test anxiety.

Questions written to measure understanding require students to apply information in new situations, to understand how concepts relate to each other, and to use information to evaluate the truth of statements. There is no substitute for understanding the material. The best thing you can do to improve your score is to study until you thoroughly understand the material. Sometimes, however, you will be faced with challenging alternatives, or with an essay question that requires you to think differently than you had anticipated. One way to prepare for tests is to practice with the same variety of questions you will encounter on your tests. Therefore, practice test items in the formats frequently encountered on tests are provided in this study guide.

1. Multiple-choice items. In general, a good strategy for taking tests consisting of multiple-choice items is to first go through the test and answer all the questions you can. Be sure to read the entire question and each alternative carefully. By responding to the items you know, you can help reduce some of the anxiety that tests evoke, and you may see alternatives that will help you answer more difficult items. However, if you are using an answer sheet that can be optically scanned, be sure that the response you select corresponds to the number of the item on the answer sheet. Also, be sure to pace yourself throughout the test. A good rule of thumb is to try to answer five multiple-choice items about every five minutes. Everyone has a unique test-taking style, and most students continue to show improvement in test-taking skill with experience.

Multiple-choice items have three parts: 1) a stem that asks a question, poses a problem, or is an incomplete sentence; 2) the correct or best answer; and 3) a number of distracters or plausible alternatives. Your task is to identify the correct or best answer among the given alternatives. Do not count on being able to answer multiple-choice items correctly merely by recognizing the correct answer. In multiple-choice questions, it is possible for every alternative to be familiar. Read each stem carefully and note particular words, like "always" and "not" to help you identify the best answer. As you approach an item, try to anticipate the answer before reading the alternatives. When you are ready to read the alternatives, always read all of them carefully before selecting the best answer.

Sometimes you simply cannot determine the best or correct alternative. If you must guess, do so after eliminating one or two alternatives. Your chances of guessing correctly improve with each alternative you are able to eliminate. If you are not penalized for guessing incorrectly, you should respond to every item. If you can eliminate all except two alternatives, ask yourself how the two answers are different. Then read the item again and try to determine if the difference is important to the item. Read the item with each separate answer. This process can reduce the distracting effect of incorrect answers and make it easier for you to make a decision about the best answer.

2. True-False Items. True-false items are used to test mastery of detailed information. Consider the following factors when responding to these items.
    a. Only Two Options. If you do not know the answer, guess. With true-false items, you have a 50-50 chance of guessing correctly.
    b. True Means Always True, False Means Always False. If a given answer is *true,* it must be true under every circumstance. Test the accuracy of statements by trying to think of examples of when the statement is false.

c. Qualifiers. If a statement is qualified (e.g., includes words like some, many, usually, frequently), this may be a cue that it is true.

d. Check Names and Dates. Details such as names and dates can easily be listed incorrectly to test your knowledge of who did what and when.

3. Matching Sets. Read the directions for matching sets because you may be permitted to re-use responses, or extra responses that will not be used may be included. If you determine that every response will be used once, you have the advantage of being able to use the process of elimination to simplify guessing from among any remaining responses.

    a. Look for Relationships. Often one column is devoted to terms, and the other to definitions for the terms. Determine whether this or another relationship is present in the set before proceeding because it may help you eliminate responses.

    b. Save Time. It takes less time to read a long definition and scan a list of short terms for a match than *vice versa*. Therefore, if a matching set includes lengthy definitions that are to be matched with short terms, read the longer definitions first.

    c. Start with What You Know. If you are not confident about the response that should go with a given item, skip it, and return to it later. The process of eliminating responses for matches about which you are confident may make it easier to decide from among remaining responses later.

4. Essay Items. In some classes, a pool of essay items from which one or more will be selected will be made available to students. In this situation, you have no excuse for not preparing thoroughly. In other classes, you may get hints about particular content on which to focus when preparing for the essay portion of a test. Take note of these hints. If you have no such direction, try some of the methods as you prepare. As you study your text, you will note that some material seems to lend itself well to objective (i.e., multiple-choice or matching) items, while other material does not. If a portion of a chapter contains information that is more easily described in narrative text than in discrete definitions, or if there are important concepts or relationships between and among concepts, this material may lend itself to writing good essay items.

Students often are able to anticipate broad topics that can be addressed in essay items. Practice reviewing the text and writing essay items of the same format and style that you encounter on tests in your class. You will get better at anticipating with practice. Once you have generated a list of potential items, outline responses to each item. Include any key words or examples that would be useful for communicating your understanding of the topic or relationship in your outline. It is not necessary to write the whole answer in longhand if you can include all the topics and elements in your outline. Study the outlines as you prepare for the test. In addition:

    1. Know the Directions. Read the directions for the essay section carefully. Sometimes grammatically correct responses are expected; other times lists are acceptable. If you are unsure, ask. Pay attention to whether you are directed to answer each item, or a subset of the items. Determine how many points ach item is worth, and be sure to respond to the more valuable items first.

    2. Make Brief Notes. Take a few minutes to make comments on scratch paper or in the margins about things you want to include in your response to each essay item. Use these notes to compose a brief outline or diagram that describes the flow of your response. This outline or diagram will help keep you from having to erase, delete, or reorganize major portions of your essay. A well-organized, legible essay may earn a higher score than one that is wordy, hard to follow and difficult to read.

    3. Budget Your Time, and Stay on Schedule. Unless you have been granted unlimited time to complete a test, you will need to monitor the time that is available for responding. If each item you are to answer is of equal length and complexity, distribute your time evenly. You may want to allocate more time to an item if it is weighted more heavily, or if your response will require more detailed information. Be sure to allow time to reread your essay. A careful review of your response should help minimize grammatical errors and omissions.

    4. Reread Your Essay. When you have finished your test, reread the essay questions. If you write more than one essay, finish writing each one before editing your work. As you read, ask yourself the following questions: Are my ideas presented clearly? Did I make good use of transitional sentences? Are there any sentence fragments? Are there subject-verb agreement errors? Is the language gender- or culture-biased? Have I used effective examples to illustrate my points?

Things to Do Before the Test

1. Be Prepared. Preparation for tests can be overwhelming and should be broken into manageable units. Identify testing days on your calendar and set specific preparation goals that maximize your use of available time. By starting early, and proceeding only after mastering each unit along the way, you will save yourself a great deal of anxiety and frustration as the testing day draws nearer.

2. Be Early. Be early to every class meeting, but be especially early on testing days. When you are running late, you will be more anxious. By being early, you will be able to make full use of the time available for taking the test. It is unreasonable to ask for additional time on a test if you are not on time.

3. Stake Your Claim. You will learn about state-dependent learning in Chapter 7 of the textbook. State-, mood-, and context-dependent learning can facilitate recall of information at test time. While the effects of any of these may not be very great, anything that helps is important. If your goal is to perform well, you will want to take advantage of anything that might facilitate your performance. In general, you want to maintain the same conditions at retrieval time that were in place when information was encoded. Consider the following suggestions:

    a. Keep Your Physiological State Constant. Do not drink more coffee prior to a test than you drink before regular class meetings. By changing your physiological state, you disrupt normal functioning, and you may not be sensitive to feedback that would normally help cue recall. What is more, you will be distracted by the changes in your bodily activity.

    b. The Same Goes for Mood. There are data that indicate that some learning is mood-dependent. Thus, do not show up on test day angry, anxious, or otherwise upset, unless you are that way on regular class days. Maintaining an even temper and stable mood will serve you well in many facets of life.

    c. Keep Your Seat. By keeping your normal classroom seat, you are holding constant the contextual cues from the environment. Since those cues are part of a context where you think and learn about the course material, they may help improve your performance on test day.

    4. Know Your Professor's Style. Whenever possible, review samples of the test items your professor has used in the past. Getting these may be as simple as asking her or him if there is a test file you may review, or if he or she would share some sample items so you can become better acquainted with his or her style. Other students who have taken a course from your professor previously may also help. Get as much information as possible that will help you prepare for the test. If multiple choice items will be included, will they focus on definitions, or should you know how to *apply* what you have learned? Will you have to solve analogy problems? In general, your preparations should match the type of test you will take. Learn to anticipate test items, and practice responding to them. This study guide will help you.

5. Recognition Is Easier than Comprehension. Do not convince yourself that you understand material just because you recognize from textbooks or from class presentations. Good books make the most difficult material accessible to students who are new to the field, and good teachers can make challenging concepts seem easy to understand. Beware that although you may absorb material as you read or hear it, additional effort may be required to comprehend it fully. Challenge yourself to recall as much as possible about a given topic without cues from your textbook or notes.

Comment on Returned Objective Tests

After you have taken a test and received your test score, be sure to make an appointment with the professor to go over the test. Look for patterns in the test items that you missed. Do not be too hard on yourself. You cannot possibly know the answer to every item. Remember that your aim is to do the best that you can and to find ways to improve your test scores over time. If you know that you will receive your test after it has been graded, make notes beside each item that will remind you why you selected an alternative. Following tests, determine what you can do to improve your preparation for objective tests, and how you can improve the quality of your essays responses through preparation and planning.

CHAPTER 1

Psychology, Research, and You

Notes from Class and the Textbook

Use the space provided in this outline to record notes from the textbook, as well as from class lectures and discussion. The *Psychological Detective, Hands On, Myth or Science* and *Study Tip* sections in the textbook are included in the outline, and space is provided for you to respond to the questions or complete the activities described in these sections. Again, the icons for these sections are:

Psychological Detective

Hands On

Myth or Science

Study Tip

I. Becoming a Psychological Detective

    A. Arthur Conan Doyle's Belief in Fairies

        1. The Law of Parsimony

    B. Guidelines for the Psychological Detective

        1. What is the statement or claim, and who is making it?

Consider the *Study Tip* on p. 6 in the textbook.

      2.   Is the statement or claim based on scientific observations?

      3.   What do statistics reveal?

      4.   Are there plausible alternative explanations for the statement or claim?

Consider the *Study Tip* on p. 7 in the textbook.

II. Research Methods in Psychology

      A. The Case Study

      B. Naturalistic Observation

      C. Correlational Research

Complete the *Hands On* activity on pp. 12-13 in the textbook.

Consider the *Psychological Detective* activity on p. 13 in the textbook.

D. Survey Research

Consider the *Psychological Detective* activity on p. 14 in the textbook.

E. Qualitative Research

F. The Experimental Method

Consider the *Psychological Detective* activity on p. 17 in the textbook.

G. Statistics and Psychologists

Consider the *Psychological Detective* activity on p. 18 in the textbook.

4

1. Descriptive Statistics

Consider the *Psychological Detective* activity on p. 19 in the textbook.

2. Inferential Statistics

H. Research Ethics

1. Protection from Harm

2. Confidentiality

3. Voluntary Participation

4. Deception and Intimidation

5. The Ethics of Research with Animals

Consider the *Study Tip* on p. 20 in the textbook.

III. The Origins of Modern Psychology

    A.   Wundt and Structuralism

    B.   Functionalism

    C.   Gestalt Psychology

    D.   The Behavioral Perspective

    E. Sigmund Freud and the Psychodynamic Perspective

    F. The Humanistic Perspective

    G. The Physiological Perspective

    H. The Evolutionary Perspective

    I. The Cognitive Perspective

    J. The Cultural and Diversity Perspective

    K. The Environmental, Population, and Conservation Perspective

Consider the *Study Tip* on p. 30 in the textbook.

IV. Present-Day Psychology

V. Psychological Specialties

    A. Clinical and Counseling Psychology

    B. Other Specialties

Consider the *Psychological Detective* activity on p. 34 in the textbook.

    C. Emerging Specialties

Chapter Test

In addition to completing the practice items that follow, you should be sure to complete the items in the *Check Your Progress* sections in each chapter of the textbook. The answers to the **Multiple Choice Items**, **Completion Items**, and **Critical Thinking Exercises** are presented at the end of the **Chapter Test**.

Multiple Choice Items

Circle the letter that corresponds to the *best* alternative for each of the following items.

1. An unintentional influence on the results of an experiment is
   a. an observation.
   b. an independent variable.
   c. a placebo.
   d. a bias.

2. The principle that the simplest explanation of a phenomenon is preferred to a more complex explanation is a statement of
   a. eclecticism.
   b. a gestalt.
   c. a testable hypothesis.
   d. the law of parsimony.

3. Like all scientists, psychologists employ the scientific method to investigate phenomena because it involves
   a. microscopes, beakers, and similar scientific apparatus.
   b. summarizing findings into widely applicable laws of behavior.
   c. using theories to derive hypotheses which may be tested experimentally.
   d. challenging daily the claims made by popular press information sources.

4. A prediction about future behavior derived from observation and theory is
    a. a hypothesis.
    b. naturalistic observation.
    c. an experimental design.
    d. an operational definition.

5. The experimental method is a preferred means of gathering information because it
    a. is easy to use in most research contexts.
    b. can provide the basis for cause-and-effect statements.
    c. has a name that conveys credibility, and credibility is the primary goal of psychological research.
    d. is a fairly inexpensive technique when compared with other approaches (e.g., naturalistic observation).

6. A research project yielded statistically significant data indicating that first year college students who took introductory psychology scored higher on a problem-solving test than did a comparable group of students who did not enroll in introductory psychology. According to this statement,
    a. students should take psychology if they get the chance.
    b. psychology students are smarter than non-psychology students.
    c. even though the psychology students did statistically better, they did not perform absolutely better.
    d. psychology students outperformed non-psychology students at a level greater than would be predicted by chance alone.

7. A psychologist who has created a scatterplot of data collected in an experiment is planning to
    a. identify a placebo effect.
    b. eliminate an extraneous variable.
    c. calculate a correlation coefficient.
    d. determine a cause and effect relationship.

8. A sample of people selected so that it reflects the characteristics of the population of interest to the investigator is said to be
    a. random.
    b. representative.
    c. biased.
    d. operational.

9. Case studies and naturalistic observation are similar in that
    a. data from both generalize well in other contexts.
    b. both have limitations but are useful in developing research ideas.
    c. with each method, participants are scarcely aware they are being studied.
    d. naturalistic observation involves essentially several concurrent case studies.

10. The correlation coefficient that indicates the strongest degree of relationship between two variables is
    a. $r = -0.8$
    b. $r = -0.2$
    c. $r = +0.1$
    d. $r = +0.75$

11. A psychologist who conducts several focus groups of high school students to learn whether a uniform dress code has reduced the number of cliques in the school is conducting
    a. experimental research.
    b. survey research.
    c. case study research.
    d. qualitative research.

12. If a psychologist uses the experimental method to determine whether group therapy is as effective as individual therapy in treating test anxiety, this type of therapy is the
   a. independent variable.
   b. dependent variable.
   c. extraneous variable.
   d. confounding variable.

13. If an experiment includes a group that is not exposed to the independent variable, the group is the
   a. control group.
   b. representative sample.
   c. case group.
   d. focus group.

14. In Bandura's study of the effects of modeling on aggression, the dependent variable was
   a. the population of nursery school children.
   b. the age in months of the children in the study.
   c. the number of times participants hit the Bobo doll.
   d. systematic exposure to either the aggressive model or the nonaggressive model.

15. In Bandura's study of the effects of modeling on aggression, the independent variable was
   a. the population of nursery school children.
   b. the age in months of the children in the study.
   c. the number of times participants hit the Bobo doll.
   d. systematic exposure to either the aggressive model or the nonaggressive model.

16. Defining aggression as the number of times one child pushes or hits other children in a 5-minute period is an example of
   a. an operational definition.
   b. a hypothesis.
   c. an explanation.
   d. a theory.

17. Psychologists who use the experimental method manipulate ___ variables, control for ___ variables, and measure changes in ___ variables
   a. dependent; independent; extraneous.
   b. extraneous; dependent; independent.
   c. independent; extraneous; dependent.
   d. dependent; extraneous; independent.

18. Using the random assignment is one way
   a. to ensure a proper control group.
   b. to control for extraneous variability.
   c. to really mess up an experiment, all assignments should be nonrandom.
   d. to scramble the independent and dependent variables and to help guard against bias.

19. A psychologist who wants to use statistics to determine whether the independent variable has had an effect will use
   a. descriptive statistics.
   b. measures of central tendency.
   c. measures of variability.
   d. inferential statistics.

20. Prior to being enrolled in a psychological study, the specific procedures that all participants will undergo and any risks that will be encountered are described so that potential participants can
    a. be debriefed.
    b. be assured that confidentiality will be maintained.
    c. give their informed consent.
    d. identify evidence of experimenter deception.

21. The process of informing all participants about the purpose of an investigation and explaining why particular methods were used is
    a. debriefing.
    b. confidentiality.
    c. informed consent.
    d. deception.

22. Wundt's original studies were designed to
    a. describe the contents of the unconscious mind.
    b. study the contents of the conscious mind.
    c. focus the study of behavior on that which was overtly observable.
    d. challenge the notion that conscious experience could be broken down into elements.

23. James' studies were designed to
    a. describe the contents of the unconscious mind.
    b. study the purposes of consciousness.
    c. focus the study of behavior on that which was overtly observable.
    d. challenge the notion that conscious experience could be broken down into elements.

24. A Gestalt psychologist would agree with the statement that
    a. most behavior is determined by unconscious processes.
    b. individuals have free will and are in control of their own behavior.
    c. only overt behavior is interesting because mental processes cannot be observed.
    d. the whole is greater than the sum of its parts.

25. A humanist psychologist would agree with the statement that
    a. most behavior is determined by unconscious processes.
    b. individuals have free will and are in control of their own behavior.
    c. only overt behavior is interesting because mental processes cannot be observed.
    d. the whole is greater than the sum of its parts.

26. A psychologist investigating the way students store information in memory and retrieve it is exhibiting the
    a. evolutionary perspective.
    b. behavioral perspective.
    c. cognitive perspective.
    d. psychodynamic perspective.

27. The psychological specialty concerned with diagnosing and treating psychological disorders is
    a. forensic psychology.
    b. neuropsychology.
    c. sport psychology.
    d. clinical psychology.

28. An actor portraying a psychologist in an episode of CSI: Miami is a
    a. cross-cultural psychologist.
    b. school psychologist.
    c. clinical psychologist.
    d. forensic psychologist.

29. A psychologist conducting a survey to obtain information for a mail order company about current public attitudes toward credit purchases is practicing
   a. cross-cultural psychology.
   b. consumer psychology.
   c. clinical psychology.
   d. forensic psychology.

30. A psychologist helping a patient who has had a heart attack adjust to the aftereffects of surgery is a
   a. cross-cultural psychologist.
   b. health psychologist.
   c. clinical psychologist.
   d. forensic psychologist.

Completion Items
Complete the following statements with key terms or concepts from the textbook. Answer as many as you can without referring to your notes or to the book. If you have blanks after thinking about each item, try using your book.

1. A person taking a capsule filled with saline solution who reports felling better is experiencing a _____.

2. An explanation for a behavior based on careful, precise observation is a _____.

3. An in-depth study of a single individual is a _____.

4. A psychologist who observes high school student interactions at a mall to learn more about the formation of social groups is conducting a _____.

5. The group in an experiment that does not receive the independent variable is the _____ group.

6. The group in an experiment that does receive the independent variable is the _____ group.

7. Variables other than the independent variable that can influence the outcome of an experiment are _____.

8. Statistical procedures used to summarize any set of data are _____ statistics.

9. Statistical procedures used to analyze data after an experiment has been completed are _____ statistics.

10. Statistics that provide information about typical scores in a set of data are measures of _____.

11. Statistics that indicate the spread of scores in a set of data are measures of _____.

12. The method used by structural psychologists in which participants reported the contents of their conscious experience is _____.

13. The psychological perspective that focuses only on observable behavior and emphasizes the learned nature of behavior is the _____ perspective.

14. The view that normal and abnormal behaviors are determined primarily by unconscious forces is the _____ perspective.

15. Interest in the role that physiological structures or behavior play in helping an organism adapt to its environment is characteristic of the _____ perspective.

16. The difference between psychologists and psychiatrists is that the latter have earned a _____ degree.

17. A psychologist whose approach to therapy combines practices from behavioral, cognitive, and humanistic psychology uses an _____ approach.

18. The view that all other cultures are extensions of one's own culture is _____.

19. A psychologist observed administering a battery of tests to determine why a child is reversing letters like "b" and "d" is a _____ psychologist.

20. A psychologist who works with war veterans to help them overcome the effects of severe head injuries is a _____ .

Critical Thinking Exercises

Which research method(s) would a psychologist use to answer the following questions?

1. What is the relationship between the number of credit hours college students take and their grade point average (GPA)?

2. What would lead a person to become a serial killer?

3. How many drivers exceed the speed limit on a highway leading to the university on a typical weekday?

4. Does the presence of music cause shoppers to buy more products in department stores?

5. How many people believe in psychic phenomena?

Critical thinking about correlations
How are these variables related to one another? What type of correlation, positive, negative or zero correlation, would you predict with these variables?

Variables to compare	Correlation type
Weight loss per month and time spent watching TV per week	
Average speed of an automobile and amount of gasoline purchased for a car per month	
Calories consumed per week and an automobile's average miles per gallon	
Age and weight loss per month	

Chapter Test Answers
Multiple Choice Items

1. d	11. d	21. a
2. d	12. a	22. b
3. c	13. a	23. b
4. a	14. c	24. d
5. b	15. d	25. b
6. d	16. a	26. c
7. c	17. c	27. d
8. b	18. b	28. d
9. b	19. d	29. b
10. a	20. c	30. b

Completion Items

1. placebo effect	11. variability
2. theory	12. introspection
3. case study	13. behavioral
4. naturalistic observation	14. psychodynamic
5. control group	15. evolutionary
6. experimental group	16. medical
7. extraneous variables	17. eclectic
8. descriptive	18. ethnocentrism
9. inferential	19. school
10. central tendency	20. neuropsychologist

Critical Thinking Exercises

1. A correlational study would be used to determine the relationship between the number of credit hours in college and grade point average.
2. A case study could be used to identify factors that might lead someone to become a serial killer.
3. Using a radar gun, a naturalistic observation study could be used to count the number of drivers who exceed the speed limit.
4. An experimental design would be used to determine whether music causes shoppers to buy more products.
5. A descriptive method such as a survey could be used to determine the number of people who believe in psychic phenomena.

Correlations

Variables to compare	Correlation type
Weight loss per month and time spent watching TV per week	Negative correlation: as time spent watching TV increases, weight loss decreases
Average speed of an automobile and amount of gasoline purchased for car per month	Positive correlation: as automobile speed, gasoline use increases
Calories consumed per week and an automobile's average mpg	Zero correlation: there is no relationship between calories consumed and automobile mpg
Age and weight loss per month	Negative correlation because as we get older, we tend to have more difficulty losing weight. However, there are exceptions in that the oldest old tend to lose weight.

Key Vocabulary Terms: The terms listed in the margins of pages and entered in **boldface** type in the textbook are listed below with space for you to write the definitions. You may also want to create a list of the terms entered in italics in the textbook, especially those your instructor mentions in lectures. You should try to write definitions *in your own words* because translating the terms into familiar language will facilitate retention.

psychology

bias

law of parsimony

placebo effect

scientific method

theory

hypothesis

case study

naturalistic observation

scatterplot

correlation coefficient

survey method

representative sample

qualitative research

experimental method

independent variable (IV)

dependent variable (DV)

operational definition

experimental group

control group

extraneous variables

random assignment

statistics

descriptive statistics

inferential statistics

measures of central tendency

measures of variability

informed consent

debriefing

structuralism

introspection

cognitive psychology

functionalism

Gestalt psychology

behavioral perspective

psychodynamic perspective

psychoanalytic therapy

humanistic perspective

physiological perspective

evolutionary perspective

cognitive perspective

environmental, population, and conservation perspective

eclectic approach

clinical psychology

psychiatrist

counseling psychology

research psychologist

ethnocentrism

cross-cultural psychology

school psychologist

industrial and organizational (I/O) psychologist

consumer psychology

health psychology

forensic psychologist

sport psychologist

neuropsychologist

CHAPTER 2

Behavioral Neuroscience

Notes from Class and the Textbook

Use the space provided in this outline to record notes from the textbook as well as from class lectures and discussion.

I. Biology and Behavior

    A. Evolutionary Psychology

Consider the *Psychological Detective* activity on p. 42 in the textbook.

    B. The Evolutionary Perspective

II. The Nervous System

    A. The Peripheral Nervous System

        1. The Somatic Division

        2. The Autonomic Division

        3. The Sympathetic System

Consider the *Psychological Detective* activity on pp. 44-45 in the textbook.

        4. The Parasympathetic System

B. The Central Nervous System

    1. The Spinal Cord

Consider the *Study Tip* on p. 45 in the textbook.

III. The Endocrine System

    A. Major Endocrine Glands

        1.   The Pineal Gland

        2.   The Pancreas

        3.   Hypothalamus

        4.   The Pituitary Gland

        5.   The Thyroid Gland

        6.   The Gonads

        7.   The Adrenal Glands

    B. The Relation of the Endocrine System and the Nervous System

Consider the *Study Tip* on p. 49 in the textbook.

IV. Neurons: Basic Cells of the Nervous System

    A. Components of the Neuron

        1. The Myelin Sheath

    B. The Synapse and Neurotransmitters

        1. The Synapse

Consider the *Psychological Detective* activity on p. 55 in the textbook.

        2. Dopamine

        3. Serotonin

        4. Acetylcholine

5. Glutamate

6. GABA

7. Norepinephrine

Consider the *Study Tip* on p. 56 in the textbook.

8. Clearing the Synapse

9. Neurotransmitters and Drug Action

10. Agonists

11. Antagonists

12. Neuromodulators

C. The Neural Signal

V. The Brain: A Closer Look

    A. Investigating Brain Functioning

        1. The Case Study Method

        2. Stereotaxic Surgery

        3. The Electroencephalograph

        4. Alpha Waves

        5. Beta Waves

        6. Theta Waves

        7. Delta Waves

        8. Computerized Brain Imaging

Consider the *Psychological Detective* activity on p. 67 in the textbook.

    B. Major Components of the Brain

        1. The Hindbrain

2. The Midbrain

3. The Forebrain

4. Frontal Lobes

5. Parietal Lobes

Complete the *Myth or Science* activity on p. 75 in the textbook.

6. Temporal Lobes

7. Occipital Lobes

8. Language and the Brain

C. The Split Brain

Consider the *Psychological Detective* activity on pp. 77-78 in the textbook.

D. Neuroplasticity: The Modifiable Brain

Consider the *Study Tip* on p. 78 in the textbook.

Chapter Test

In addition to completing the practice items that follow, remember to complete the items in the *Check Your Progress* sections in each chapter of the textbook. The answers to the **Multiple Choice Items**, **Completion Items**, and **Critical Thinking Exercises** are presented at the end of the **Chapter Test**.

Multiple Choice Items

Circle the letter that corresponds to the ***best*** alternative for each of the following items.

1. The question psychologists who have an evolutionary perspective ask is
    a. "How does a person survive in today's world?"
    b. "Why does dysfunctional behavior persist over generations?"
    c. "Which physiological and biological structures developed over generations?"
    d. "What role does a given structure or behavior have in survival and adaptation?"

2. The brain and spinal cord comprise the
    a. central nervous system.
    b. peripheral nervous system.
    c. autonomic nervous system.
    d. parasympathetic nervous system.

3. All the neural fibers lying outside the central nervous system comprise the
    a. central nervous system.
    b. peripheral nervous system.
    c. autonomic nervous system.
    d. parasympathetic nervous system.

4. Breathing, heart rate, and digestion are controlled by the
    a. central nervous system.
    b. peripheral nervous system.
    c. autonomic nervous system.
    d. parasympathetic nervous system.

5. If a person accidentally touches a hot burner on a stove, the division of the peripheral nervous system that conducts the pain message from the skin to the brain is the
    a. central nervous system.
    b. peripheral nervous system.
    c. somatic nervous system.
    d. parasympathetic nervous system.

6. If a person accidentally touches a hot burner on a stove, the nerves that carry information from the brain instructing the muscles in the arm to move the finger away from the hot burner are
    a. afferent nerves.
    b. efferent nerves.
    c. glial cells.
    d. interneurons.

7. The behavior involved in moving the finger away from the hot burner is
    a. reticulation.
    b. apraxia.
    c. a reflex.
    d. a cognition.

8. The arousal experienced by a person who suddenly finds himself driving the wrong way on a busy one-way street is primarily due to activation of the
    a. central nervous system.
    b. peripheral nervous system.
    c. sympathetic nervous system.
    d. parasympathetic nervous system.

9. After turning around on a one-way street without causing a wreck, the body returns to a resting or balanced state due to activation of the
    a. central nervous system.
    b. peripheral nervous system.
    c. sympathetic nervous system.
    d. parasympathetic nervous system.

10. The endocrine gland that plays an important role in the development of diabetes is the
    a. pineal gland.
    b. pancreas.
    c. the thyroid gland.
    d. thalamus.

11. The endocrine gland referred to as the master gland is the
    a. pituitary gland.
    b. pancreas.
    c. the thyroid gland.
    d. thalamus.

12. The adrenal glands play an important role in activation of
    a. diabetes
    b. reproduction.
    c. the "fight or flight" response.
    d. the metabolic rate.

13. The speed of neural conduction is increased by
    a. glial cells.
    b. agonists.
    c. dendrites.
    d. the synapse.

14. Interaction between two neurons occurs at the
    a. myelin sheath.
    b. dendrites.
    c. soma.
    d. synapse.

15. Drugs like Haldol that block the receptors for specific neurotransmitters like dopamine are called
    a. agonists.
    b. antagonists.
    c. neuromodulators.
    d. endorphins.

16. Drugs like morphine that have a general effect on the release of neurotransmitters are called
    a. agonists.
    b. antagonists.
    c. neuromodulators.
    d. endorphins.

17. Substances produced by the body that reduce pain and induce feelings of exhilaration are called
    a. agonists.
    b. antagonists.
    c. neuromodulators.
    d. endorphins.

18. The reversal of the electrical charge of a neuron when it fires is its
    a. action potential.
    b. resting state.
    c. refractory period.
    d. polarization state.

19. The technique used to study the metabolic activity of the brain is
    a. positron emission tomography.
    b. computerized axial tomography.
    c. magnetic resonance imaging.
    d. functional magnetic resonance imaging.

20. The technique used to study the brain based on computerized interpretation of a large number of X-rays is
    a. the electroencephalograph.
    b. computerized axial tomography.
    c. magnetic resonance imaging.
    d. functional magnetic resonance imaging.

21. The part of the brain responsible for basic survival activities is the
    a. medulla.
    b. reticular formation.
    c. brain stem.
    d. corpus callosum.

22. The two hemispheres of the brain are connected by the
    a. medulla.
    b. reticular formation.
    c. brain stem.
    d. corpus callosum.

23. The activity controlled by the limbic system is
    a. higher order cognition.
    b. sensory integration.
    c. voluntary movement.
    d. emotional reactivity.

24. The activity controlled by the frontal lobes is
    a. decision making.
    b. sensory integration.
    c. voluntary movement.
    d. emotional reactivity.

25. A person who suffers a severe injury to the parietal lobes would experience deficits in
    a. higher order cognition.
    b. sensory integration.
    c. understanding speech.
    d. emotional reactivity.

26. A person who suffers a severe injury to the temporal lobes would experience deficits in
    a. higher order cognition.
    b. sensory integration.
    c. understanding speech.
    d. emotional reactivity.

27. A person who has difficulty processing visual stimuli has suffered injury to the
    a. frontal lobes.
    b. reticular formation.
    c. corpus callosum.
    d. occipital lobes.

28. A person diagnosed with aphasia will have difficulty
    a. seeing.
    b. dressing.
    c. speaking.
    d. hearing.

29. A person diagnosed with apraxia will have difficulty
    a. seeing.
    b. dressing.
    c. speaking.
    d. hearing.

30. The fact that the brain can adapt to the extent that a function like hearing can be assumed by another area following severe injury to the temporal lobes is evidence of
    a. action potential.
    b. natural selection.
    c. neuromodulation.
    d. neuroplasticity.

Completion Items

Provide the missing information in the diagrams that follow.

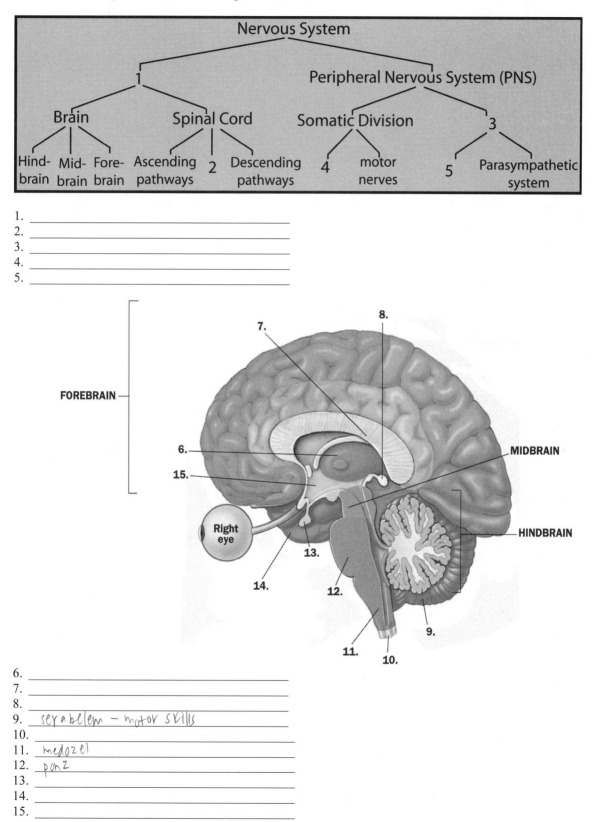

1. _____
2. _____
3. _____
4. _____
5. _____

6. _____
7. _____
8. _____
9. serabelem — motor skills
10. _____
11. medozel
12. ponz
13. _____
14. _____
15. _____

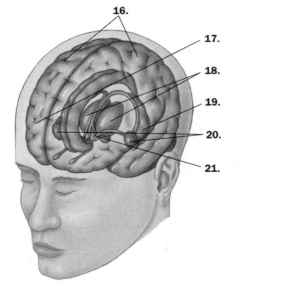

16. _____
17. _____
18. _____
19. _____
20. _____
21. _____

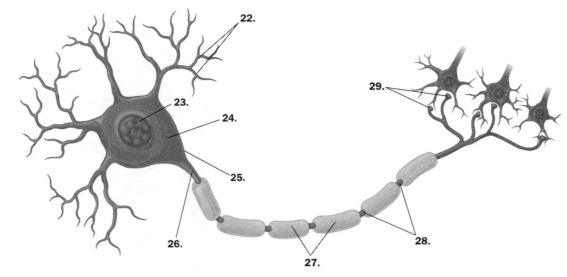

22. _____
23. _____
24. _____
25. _____
26. _____
27. _____
28. _____
29. _____

Chapter Test Answers
Multiple Choice Items

1. d	11. a	21. c
2. a	12. c	22. d
3. b	13. a	23. d
4. c	14. d	24. a
5. c	15. b	25. b
6. b	16. c	26. c
7. c	17. d	27. d
8. c	18. a	28. c
9. d	19. a	29. b
10. b	20.c	30.d

Completion Items

1. central nervous system (CNS)	11. medulla	21. hypothalamus
2. interneurons	12. pons	22. dendrites
3. autonomic division	13. pituitary gland	23. cell nucleus
4. sensory nerves	14. temporal lobe	24. cell body (soma)
5. sympathetic system	15. hypothalamus	25. cell membrane
6. thalamus	16. cerebral cortex	26. axon
7. corpus callosum	17. frontal lobe	27. myelin sheath
8. pineal gland	18. thalamus	28. nodes of Ranvier
9. cerebellum	19. hippocampus	29. terminal buttons
10. spinal cord	20. amygdala	

Key Vocabulary Terms: The terms listed in the margins of pages and entered in **boldface** type in the textbook are listed below with space for you to write the definitions. Remember that you may also want to create a list of the terms entered in italics in the textbook, especially those your instructor mentions in lectures. Again, you should try to write definitions *in your own words* because translating the terms into familiar language will facilitate retention.

evolutionary psychology

natural selection

behavioral neuroscience

stimulus

receptors

central nervous system (CNS)

peripheral nervous system (PNS)

neurons

somatic nervous system

afferent (sensory) nerves

efferent (motor) nerves

autonomic nervous system

sympathetic nervous system

parasympathetic nervous system

reflex

endocrine system

hormones

pancreas

hypothalamus

pituitary gland

thyroid gland

gonads

ovaries

testes

adrenal glands

dendrite

soma

axon

terminal buttons

myelin sheath

glial cell

synapse

neurotransmitters

agonists

antagonists

neuromodulators

endorphins

resting state

action potential

electroencephalograph (EEG)

positron emission tomography (PET)

computerized axial tomography (CT or CAT)

magnetic resonance imaging (MRI)

functional magnetic resonance imaging (fMRI)

hindbrain

medulla (medulla oblongata)

pons

cerebellum

midbrain

brain stem

reticular formation

forebrain

corpus callosum

cerebral cortex (cerebrum)

limbic system

thalamus

frontal lobes

parietal lobes

temporal lobes

occipital lobes

aphasia

apraxia

CHAPTER 3

Sensation and Perception

Notes from Class and the Textbook
Use the space provided in this outline to record notes from the textbook as well as from class lectures and discussion.

Consider the *Study Tip* on p. 84 in the textbook.

I. Sensation, Perception, and Psychophysics

    A. Sensation and Perception

    B. Psychophysics

    C. Thresholds
        1. Absolute and Differential Thresholds

        2. Subliminal Perception

II. Sensory Systems

    A. Vision

        1. What We See: The Visual Stimulus

Consider the *Psychological Detective* activity on p. 88 in the textbook.

2. How We See: The Visual System

Consider the *Psychological Detective* activity on p. 92 in the textbook.

3. The Visual Pathway

4. The Visual Receptors

Consider the *Psychological Detective* activity on p. 93 in the textbook.

5. Theories of Color Vision

6. Color Deficiencies

B. Audition (Hearing)

      1. What We Hear: The Auditory Stimulus

      2. How We Hear: The Auditory System

      3. Hearing Different Tones or Pitches

      4. Locating Sounds in Our Environment

      5. Hearing Disorders

C. The Chemical Senses: Taste and Smell

      1. Taste (Gustation)

      2. What We Taste: The Gustatory Stimulus

      3. How We Taste: The Gustatory System

Consider the *Psychological Detective* activity on p. 102 in the textbook.

      4. Smell (Olfaction)

5. What We Smell: The Olfactory Stimulus

6. How We Smell: The Olfactory System

7. Combining the Physiological and Psychological to Understand Olfactory Processing

Complete the *Myth or Science* activity on p. 105 in the textbook.

8. Men and Women

9. The Interaction of Smell and Taste

D. Somatosensory Processes

1. Vestibular Sense

2. Proprioception and Kinesthetic Sense

3. The Cutaneous Senses

4. Temperature

5. Pain

Consider the *Study Tip* on p. 108 in the textbook.

III. Perception

    A. Motivation and Attention

        1.   Motivational Influences

        2.   Attention

Complete the *Hands On* activity on p. 110 in the textbook.

    B. Basic Perceptual Abilities: Patterns and Constancies

        1.   Pattern Perception

        2.   Perceptual Constancies

        3. Shape Constancy

        4. Size Constancy

        5. Depth Perception

6. Binocular Cues

7. Monocular Cues

C. Gestalt Principles of Perceptual Organization

1. Figure and Ground

2. Principles of Grouping

D. Perception of Movement

Complete the *Hands On* activity on p. 117 in the textbook.

E. Perceptual Hypotheses and Illusions

Consider the *Psychological Detective* activity on p. 118 in the textbook.

Consider the first *Study Tip* on p.119 in the textbook.

Consider the second *Study Tip* on p.119 in the textbook.

      F. Contemporary Issues and Findings in Perception Research

            1.   Parallel Processing, Visual Search, Cell Phones, and the Application of Basic Perceptual Research

IV. Paranormal Phenomena

    A. Skeptical Scientists

    B. A Believing Public

    C. A Final Word

Chapter Test

In addition to completing the practice items that follow, remember to complete the items in the *Check Your Progress* sections in each chapter in the textbook. The answers to the **Multiple Choice Items**, **Completion Items**, and **Critical Thinking Exercises** are presented at the end of the **Chapter Test**.

Multiple Choice Items

Circle the letter that corresponds to the ***best*** alternative for each of the following items.

1. The process of seeing a large blue object describes
    a.   adaptation.
    b.   perception.
    c.   saturation.
    d.   sensation.

2. The process of identifying a large blue object as a car describes
    a.   adaptation.
    b.   perception.
    c.   saturation.
    d.   sensation.

3. The lack of awareness of a person who is unaware that he is wearing too much cologne is probably due to
   a. adaptation.
   b. transduction.
   c. Weber's law.
   d. the just noticeable difference for olfaction.

4. A person who pushes the volume button on a cell phone until she can tell that the ringer sound is louder has identified her
   a. adaptive limit.
   b. absolute threshold.
   c. telekinetic phase.
   d. the just noticeable difference.

5. A person's absolute threshold is
   a. a dangerous level of sensory stimulation.
   b. the largest amount of stimulation a person can perceive.
   c. the minimum amount of energy required for conscious recognition.
   d. the smallest amount of energy required to notice a difference 50 percent of the time.

6. The smallest amount of stimulation that must be added to or subtracted from an existing stimulus for a person to detect the change 50% of the time is the
   a. absolute threshold.
   b. differential threshold.
   c. wavelength.
   d. amplitude.

7. The ability to detect sensations below the level of conscious awareness is
   a. the absolute threshold.
   b. the difference threshold.
   c. subliminal perception.
   d. signal detection.

8. Seeing a car as blue is a function of
   a. amplitude.
   b. saturation.
   c. radiant light.
   d. reflected light.

9. A theater technician whose job involves manipulating the gels that go between light bulbs and the objects they illuminate on stage is manipulating
   a. wavelength.
   b. amplitude.
   c. radiant light.
   d. reflected light.

10. The action of the ciliary muscles to change the shape of the lens to focus vision is
   a. accommodation.
   b. adaptation.
   c. closure.
   d. saturation.

11. The theory of color vision based on the idea that perceiving blue impairs perception of yellow is the
   a. trichromatic theory.
   b. color afterimage theory.
   c. opponent-process theory.
   d. gate control theory.

12. A person who stares at a red object and then sees the object as green when the red object is removed is experiencing
    a. color afterimage.
    b. saturation.
    c. a subliminal stimulus.
    d. radiant light.

13. A monochromat sees shades of
    a. red.
    b. yellow.
    c. green.
    d. gray.

14. A dichromat has difficulty seeing
    a. yellow.
    b. gray.
    c. blue.
    d. orange.

15. The purity of a sound wave is
    a. measured in hertz.
    b. a decibel.
    c. defined by place theory.
    d. called timbre.

16. The theory that perception of different pitches is attributable to vibration of the basilar membrane at different locations is
    a. place theory.
    b. opponent-process theory.
    c. frequency theory.
    d. feature analysis theory.

17. The theory that perception of different pitches is attributable to vibration of the basilar membrane at different rates is
    a. place theory.
    b. opponent-process theory.
    c. frequency theory.
    d. feature analysis theory.

18. Conduction deafness is deafness caused by
    a. damage to the middle and outer ear.
    b. damage to the inner ear.
    c. sound transmission problems in the outer and middle ear.
    d. disease or tumors in the auditory pathways or auditory cortex.

19. Sensorineural deafness is deafness caused by
    a. damage to the middle and outer ear.
    b. damage to the inner ear.
    c. sound transmission problems in the outer and middle ear.
    d. disease or tumors in the auditory pathways or auditory cortex.

20. Taste receptors are located in the
    a. papillae.
    b. microvilli.
    c. taste buds.
    d. uvula.

21. Adjustments to bodily movement and postures are controlled by the
    a. proprioceptive sense.
    b. kinesthetic sense.
    c. cutaneous sense.
    d. vestibular sense.

22. The ability to process more than one source of stimulation at the same time is
    a. synesthesia.
    b. kinesthesia.
    c. divided attention.
    d. extrasensory perception.

23. The ability to distinguish between a square and a rectangle is attributable to
    a. feature analysis.
    b. shape constancy.
    c. binocular disparity.
    d. pattern perception.

24. The ability to recognize a door as a door, even when it is open and only edge can be seen is
    a. feature analysis.
    b. shape constancy.
    c. binocular disparity.
    d. pattern perception.

25. The process operating when a person sees one image of an object with the left eye closed and a different image with the right eye closed is
    a. binocular disparity.
    b. pattern perception.
    c. size constancy.
    d. shape constancy.

26. The Gestalt principle that smooth, flowing lines are more readily perceived than choppy, broken lines is
    a. proximity.
    b. similarity.
    c. good continuation.
    d. closure.

27. The Gestalt principle that organizing perceptions into whole objects is easier than perceiving separate parts independently is
    a. proximity.
    b. similarity.
    c. good continuation.
    d. closure.

28. The Gestalt principle that explains action in movies is
    a. apparent motion.
    b. similarity.
    c. good continuation.
    d. closure.

29. The fact that the grass does look greener on the other side of the fence is an example of
    a. a visual search.
    b. a perceptual illusion.
    c. good continuation.
    d. closure.

30. Clairvoyance, telepathy, and precognition are examples of
    a. extrasensory perception.
    b. closure.
    c. proprioceptive senses.
    d. transduction.

Completion Items

Provide the missing information in the diagrams that follow.

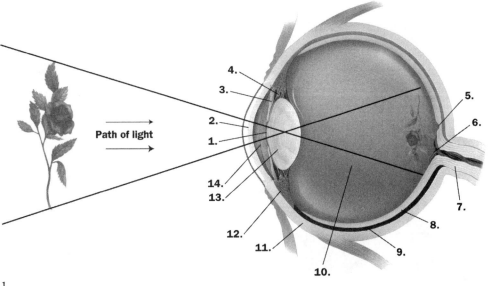

Path of light

1. _____
2. _____
3. _____
4. _____
5. _____
6. _____
7. _____
8. _____
9. _____
10. _____
11. _____
12. _____
13. _____
14. _____

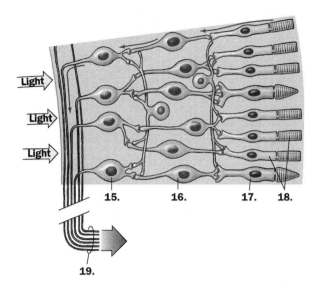

15. _____
16. _____
17. _____
18. _____
19. _____

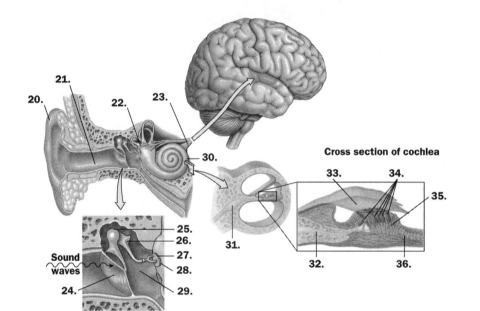

Cross section of cochlea

20. _____
21. _____
22. _____
23. _____
24. _____
25. _____

26. _____
27. _____
28. _____
29. _____
30. _____
31. _____
32. _____
33. _____
34. _____
35. _____
36. _____

Chapter Test Answers
Multiple Choice Items

1. d	11. c	21. d
2. b	12. a	22. c
3. a	13. d	23. d
4. d	14. c	24. b
5. c	15. d	25. a
6. b	16. a	26. c
7. c	17. c	27. d
8. d	18. c	28. a
9. c	19. b	29. b
10. a	20.c	30.a

Completion Items

1. Pupil	10. Vitreous humor	19. Optic nerve	28. Oval window
2. Cornea	11. Sclera	20. Pinna	29. Middle ear
3. Iris	12. Ciliary muscle	21. Ear canal	30. Cochlea
4. Ligament	13. Lens	22. Vestibular organ	31. Cochlear nerve
5.Fovea	14. Aqueous humor	23. Auditory nerve	32. Cochlear nerve fibers
6. Blind spot	15. Ganglion cell	24. Eardrum	33. Tectorial membrane
7. Optic nerve	16. Bipolar cell	25. Hammer	34. Hair cells
8. Retina	17. Cone	26. Anvil	35. Organ of Corti
9. Choroid	18. Rods	27. Stirrup	36. Basilar membrane

Key Vocabulary Terms: The terms listed in the margins of the pages and entered in **boldface** type in the textbook are listed below with space for you to write the definitions. Remember that you may also want to create a list of the terms entered in italics in the textbook, especially those your instructor mentions in lectures. Again, you should try to write definitions *in your own words* because translating the terms into familiar language will facilitate retention.

sensation

perception

transduction

adaptation

Weber's law

just noticeable difference (jnd)

absolute threshold

differential threshold

signal detection theory

subliminal stimuli

wavelength

amplitude

saturation

radiant light

reflected light

accommodation

retina

bipolar cells

ganglion cells

blind spot

optic chiasm

rods

cones

fovea

trichromatic theory

opponent-process theory

color afterimage

monochromat

dichromat

audition

hertz (Hz)

decibel (db)

timbre

ossicles

oval window

basilar membrane

organ of Corti

tectorial membrane

place theory

frequency theory

conduction deafness

sensorineural deafness

central deafness

gustation

taste buds

papillae

microvilli

olfaction

vestibular sense

semicircular canals

utricle

proprioceptive sense

kinesthetic sense

cutaneous senses

homeothermic

gate control theory

divided attention

pattern perception

feature analysis theory

perceptual constancy

shape constancy

size constancy

depth perception

binocular cues

monocular cues

binocular disparity

figure-ground relation

proximity

similarity

good continuation

closure

apparent motion

perceptual hypothesis

perceptual illusions

visual search

extrasensory perception (ESP)

CHAPTER 4

States of Consciousness

Notes from Class and the Textbook
Use the space provided in this outline to record notes from the textbook as well as from class lectures and discussion.

I. What Is Consciousness?

    A. Anesthetic Depth

    B. Brain-Injured Patients and Consciousness

II. The Rhythms of Life

    A. Circadian Rhythms

        1. The Sleep-Wake Cycle

        2. Body Temperature

Consider the *Psychological Detective* activity on p. 131 in the textbook.

Complete the *Hands On* activity on p. 132 in the textbook.

    B. Problems with Circadian Rhythms

        1. Jet Lag

Consider the *Psychological Detective* activity on p. 132 in the textbook.

       2. Shift Work

       3. Improving Shift Work

III. The Study of Sleep

Consider the *Study Tip* on p. 135 in the textbook.

    A.   A Night in a Sleep Lab

    B. The Stages of Sleep

       1. Non-REM Sleep

       2. REM Sleep

    C.   Differences in Individual Sleep Patterns

Complete the *Hands On* activity on p. 138 in the textbook.

    D.   The Functions of Sleep

Complete the *Myth or Science* activity on p. 140 in the textbook.

    E. Sleep Problems

        1. Insomnia

        2. Hypersomnias

        3. Narcolepsy

Consider the *Psychological Detective* activity on p. 142 in the textbook.

        4. Sleep Apnea

        5. Parasomnias

        6. Sleepwalking

Consider the *Psychological Detective* activity on p. 143 in the textbook.

7. Enuresis

8. Sleep Terrors and Nightmares

Consider the *Psychological Detective* activity on p. 145 in the textbook.

9. SIDS

F. Dreams: Nighttime Theater

1. Why We Forget Our Dreams

2. Culture and Dreams

3. Interpreting Dreams

IV. Hypnosis

A. The History of Hypnosis

B. Hypnotic Induction

C. Hypnotic Phenomena

1. Pain Reduction and Medical Treatment

Consider the *Psychological Detective* activity on p. 151 in the textbook.

       2.   Memory Effects

       3.   Perception

       4. Age Regression

Consider the *Psychological Detective* activity on p. 152 in the textbook.

      D. Explanations of Hypnosis

Consider the *Study Tip* on p. 153 in the textbook.

Consider the *Psychological Detective* activity on p. 153 in the textbook.

V. Altering Consciousness with Drugs

Consider the *Study Tip* on p. 157 in the textbook.

    A. Depressants

        1. Alcohol

        2. Effects of Alcohol

        3. Factors that Influence Alcohol Use

Consider the *Study Tip* on p. 160 in the textbook.

        4. Barbiturates and Benzodiazepines

    B. Stimulants

    C. Opiates

    D. Hallucinogens

        1. Lysergic acid diethylamide (LSD)

        2. Phencyclidine piperidine (PCP)

        3. Marijuana

Chapter Test

In addition to completing the practice items that follow, remember to complete the items in the *Check Your Progress* sections in each chapter in the textbook. The answers to the **Multiple Choice Items**, **Completion Items**, and **Critical Thinking Exercises** are presented at the end of the **Chapter Test**.

Multiple Choice Items

Circle the letter that corresponds to the *best* alternative for each of the following items.

1. Awareness of feelings, sensations, and thoughts at a given moment is
    a. behavior.
    b. memory.
    c. personality.
    d. consciousness.

2. A college student who experiences fantasies about attractive people while awake and sitting in class is
    a. experiencing insomnia.
    b. having hallucinations.
    c. daydreaming.
    d. dissociating.

3. An early bird's temperature will peak at
    a. 8:00am.
    b. 11:00am.
    c. 4:00pm.
    d. 8:00pm.

4. Jet lag is most severe when a person travels
    a. from west to east.
    b. from east to west.
    c. from north to south.
    d. from south to north.

5. A person awakened by a sleep researcher when the researcher notices the person's eyes moving rapidly under the eyelids is likely to
    a. be dazed and confused.
    b. say that she had not been sleeping at all.
    c. report experiencing slow-wave sleep.
    d. say that she was dreaming.

6. Evidence that sleep deprivation does have an effect on the body's functioning is evidenced by
    a. slow-wave sleep.
    b. non-REM sleep.
    c. REM sleep.
    d. REM rebound.

7. A person who complains of difficulty falling asleep and staying asleep is experiencing
    a. insomnia.
    b. narcolepsy.
    c. sleep apnea.
    d. enuresis.

8. During an intense, emotional interaction with his girlfriend a man who suddenly loses muscle tone and falls to the ground, sound asleep is experiencing
    a. an insomnia attack.
    b. sleep apnea.
    c. cataplexy.
    d. paralysis.

9. A person experiencing sleep apnea is most likely to be
    a. a younger, overweight woman.
    b. an older woman of normal weight.
    c. a younger man of normal weight.
    d. an older, overweight man.

10. A child being treated for a sleep disorder is probably experiencing
    a. a parasomnia.
    b. dissociation.
    c. a hypersomnia.
    d. cataplexy.

11. A child who sits up in bed is experiencing
    a. enuresis.
    b. sleepwalking.
    c. a sleep terror.
    d. a nightmare.

12. A child who sits up in bed and screams is experiencing
    a. enuresis.
    b. sleepwalking.
    c. a sleep terror.
    d. a nightmare.

13. A child who is awakened by a dream is experiencing
    a. enuresis.
    b. sleepwalking.
    c. a sleep terror.
    d. a nightmare.

14. A man undergoing psychodynamic therapy who reports that in a dream, he was being attacked by a flock of birds is describing the
    a. manifest content.
    b. latent content.
    c. symbolic content.
    d. behavioral content.

15. A therapist who tells a woman undergoing psychodynamic therapy that the older woman in a dream is a mother figure is describing the
    a. manifest content.
    b. latent content.
    c. symbolic content.
    d. behavioral content.

16. The activation-synthesis hypothesis
    a. accurately predicts the behaviors of hypnotized subjects.
    b. incorporates both manifest and latent dream content as key influences.
    c. suggests that dreams are the result of cortical activation during normal REM sleep.
    d. suggests that the dream content reported by most people represents three or more combined dream reports.

17. The state of altered awareness in which a person is more susceptible to suggestions is
    a. narcolepsy.
    b. somnambulism.
    c. hypnosis.
    d. activation-synthesis.

18. A man who uses a heroin to the extent that his marriage dissolves and he loses his job because he is dangerous to himself and others is experiencing
    a. substance abuse.
    b. substance dependence.
    c. tolerance.
    d. withdrawal.

19. A woman who uses a heroin to the extent that she is considered addicted to the drug is experiencing
    a. substance abuse.
    b. substance dependence.
    c. tolerance.
    d. withdrawal.

20. A man who must drink increasing amounts of alcohol to achieve the same effect that resulted from earlier, smaller amounts has developed
    a. substance abuse.
    b. substance dependence.
    c. tolerance.
    d. withdrawal.

21. A woman who has not had her usual amount of alcohol and becomes irritable and experiences physical symptoms like sweating and palpitations is undergoing
    a. substance abuse.
    b. substance dependence.
    c. tolerance.
    d. withdrawal.

22. A drug that slows the activity of the CNS is
    a. an opiate.
    b. a depressant.
    c. a hallucinogen.
    d. a stimulant.

23. The unrecognized drug is
    a. alcohol.
    b. marijuana.
    c. LSD.
    d. PCP.

24. The correct fact about alcohol is
    a. people can drink and still be in control.
    b. women process alcohol differently than men.
    c. people can sober up quickly if they need to.
    d. beer does not contain as much alcohol as liquor.

25. A person having difficulty sleeping would have a prescription for
    a. an opiate.
    b. an amphetamine.
    c. a barbiturate.
    d. a hallucinogen.

26. A physician treating a man for narcolepsy would prescribe
    a. an opiate.
    b. an amphetamine.
    c. a barbiturate.
    d. a hallucinogen.

27. A physician treating a woman for postoperative pain would prescribe
    a. an opiate.
    b. an amphetamine.
    c. a barbiturate.
    d. a hallucinogen.

28. After collapsing at a party, a student taken to the emergency room was sweating, had dilated pupils and elevated temperature, heart rate, and blood pressure. The attending physician ordered a blood test and was likely screening for
    a. marijuana.
    b. cocaine.
    c. PCP.
    d. LSD.

29. After being extracted from his wrecked car, a man denied experiencing any pain despite several lacerations and an apparent broken arm. The man's denial of pain suggests that he may have ingested
    a. marijuana.
    b. cocaine.
    c. PCP.
    d. LSD.

30. A person who is euphoric and extremely hungry has probably been using
    a. marijuana.
    b. cocaine.
    c. PCP.
    d. LSD.

Completion Items
Complete the following statements with key terms or concepts from the textbook.

1. Internal biological changes that occur on a daily schedule are _____.

2. The temporary maladjustment of biological rhythms that occurs when a person changes time zones is _____.

3. Sleep researchers measure and record physiological changes during sleep with a _____.

4. The deep sleep characterized by delta waves is _____.

5. The sleep stage characterized by eye movement combined with muscular paralysis is _____.

6. Symptoms including difficulty falling asleep, frequent awakening, or poor-quality sleep are characteristic of _____.

7. Sleep disorders characterized by excessive daytime sleepiness are _____.

8. The sleep disorder that is dangerous because it involves pauses in breathing during sleep is _____.

9. The psychological term for "bedwetting" is _____.

10. The unexplained death of an apparently healthy infant under age 1 is _____.

11. A succession of visual and auditory images during sleep constitutes a _____.

12. The splitting of conscious awareness believed to play a role in hypnotic pain reduction is _____.

13. Chemicals that affect consciousness, perception, mood, and behavior are _____.

14. The pattern of alcohol use by one party in a relationship that might cause the other party to end the relationship is _____.

15. The popular term for substance dependence is _____.

16. When increasing dosages of a drug are needed to achieve the same effect as earlier doses, a person has developed _____.

17. Drugs that increase CNS activity are _____.

18. Drugs that cause changes in thinking, emotion, self-awareness, and perceptions are _____.

19. The colorless, odorless, and tasteless drug derived from the ergot fungus that grows on rye is _____.

20. The most commonly abused illicit drug in the United States is _____.

Critical Thinking Exercises

1. During a party, a student becomes less and less inhibited as the night progresses. By the time he and his friends are ready to leave, he appears very uncoordinated, having lost his balance and nearly fallen twice in the last 15 minutes, and he is stumbling as he walks.

   Identify the drug that may be involved

   Classify the drug by type

2. Shortly before an exam, a student who is normally very active and impulsive uses a drug that makes him feel much calmer and more mentally focused.

   Identify the drug that may be involved

   Classify the drug by type

Chapter Test Answers

Multiple Choice Items

1. d	11. b	21. d
2. c	12. c	22. b
3. a	13. d	23. a
4. a	14. a	24. b
5. d	15. b	25. c
6. d	16. c	26. b
7. a	17. c	27. a
8. c	18. a	28. d
9. d	19. b	29. c
10. a	20.c	30.a

Completion Items

1. circadian rhythms	11. dream
2. jet lag	12. dissociation
3. polysomnograph	13. psychoactive substances
4. slow-wave sleep	14. substance abuse
5.rapid eye movement (REM) sleep	15. addiction
6. insomnia	16. tolerance
7. hypersomnias	17. stimulants
8. sleep apnea	18. hallucinogens
9. enuresis	19. lysergic acid diethylamide (LSD)
10.sudden infant death syndrome (SIDS)	20. marijuana

Critical Thinking Exercises

1. Alcohol is the drug.
   Alcohol is a depressant that decreases inhibitions and impairs judgment. Therefore, the student's increasingly uninhibited behavior over the course of the evening is not surprising. Alcohol also affects the cerebellum, which is responsible for coordinated movement and balance so he is likely to have difficulty walking (Chapter 2.)

2. Ritalin, an amphetamine, is the drug.
   Children and adults with attention-deficit hyperactivity disorder may manifest high levels of activity and an inability to focus their attention. The administration of a stimulant like Ritalin that increases mental alertness by activating the brain, allows them to focus their attention, which, in turn, has a calming effect. Since stimulants tend to act quickly, the student can take the drug shortly (40-50 minutes) before his exam.

Key Vocabulary Terms: The terms listed in the margins of pages and entered in **boldface** type in the textbook are listed below with space for you to write the definitions. Remember that you may also want to create a list of the terms entered in italics in the textbook, especially those your instructor mentions in lectures. Again, you should try to write definitions *in your own words* because translating the terms into familiar language will facilitate retention.

consciousness

daydreaming

circadian rhythms

jet lag

polysomnograph

non-REM sleep

slow-wave sleep

rapid eye movement (REM) sleep

REM rebound

insomnia

hypersomnias

narcolepsy

sleep apnea

parasomnias

sleepwalking

enuresis

sleep terror

nightmare

sudden infant death syndrome (SIDS)

dream

manifest content

latent content

activation-synthesis hypothesis

hypnosis

dissociation

psychoactive substances

substance abuse

substance dependence

tolerance

withdrawal

depressants

alcohol

barbiturates

stimulants

amphetamines

opiates

hallucinogens

lysergic acid diethylamide (LSD)

phencyclidine piperidine (PCP)

marijuana

CHAPTER 5

Learning

Notes from Class and the Textbook

Use the space provided in this outline to record notes from the textbook as well as from class lectures and discussion.

I. What Is Learning?

II. Classical Conditioning

    A. The Basic Elements of Classical Conditioning

Complete the *Hands On* activity on p. 174 in the textbook.

Consider the *Psychological Detective* activity on p. 175 in the textbook.

    B. Classical Conditioning Processes

        1. Acquisition

            a. Sequence of CS-US Presentation

            b. Strength of the US

            c. Number of CS-US Pairings

        2. Extinction

3. Spontaneous Recovery

4. Generalization and Discrimination

Consider the *Psychological Detective* activity on p. 178 in the textbook.

C. Applications of Classical Conditioning: Phobias and Beyond

Consider the *Psychological Detective* activity on p. 179 in the textbook.

1. Classical Conditioning of Our Attitudes

2. Classical Conditioning and Our Motives

D. Classical Conditioning after Pavlov

1. Contingency Theory

2. Blocking

E. Evolution and Classical Conditioning: Taste-Aversion Learning and Preparedness

1. Taste Aversion

2. Cue-To-Consequence Learning

Consider the *Study Tip* activity on p. 184 in the textbook.

III. Operant Conditioning

    A. Reinforcers: The Basic Concept of Operant Conditioning

        1. Positive and Negative Reinforcers

        2. Positive and Negative Reinforcers Expressed as Contingencies

        3. Positive Reinforcement

        4. Negative Reinforcement

        5. Primary and Secondary (Conditioned) Reinforcers

    B. Beyond the Basics

        1. Shaping

Consider the *Psychological Detective* activity on p. 190 in the textbook.

        2. The Premack Principle

3. Escape and Avoidance Conditioning

4. Extinction

5. Stimulus Control

C. Schedules of Reinforcement

Consider the *Psychological Detective* activity on p. 193 in the textbook.

1. Continuous Reinforcement

2. Intermittent (Partial) Reinforcement

3. Ratio Schedules

4. Interval Schedules

Consider the *Study Tip* activity on p. 196 in the textbook.

5. The Partial Reinforcement Effect

D. Punishment: The Opposite of Reinforcement

Consider the *Psychological Detective* activity on p. 200 in the textbook.

E. Recent Advances in Operant Conditioning

1. Delayed Reinforcement and Discounting

2. Behavioral Ecology

V. Cognitive and Social Perspectives on Learning

A. The Role of Cognition

1. Insight Learning

2. Latent Learning

Consider the *Study Tip* activity on p. 205 in the textbook.

B. Observational Learning

Respond to the *Study Tip* activity on p. 208 in the textbook.

Chapter Test

In addition to completing the practice items that follow, remember to complete the items in the *Check Your Progress* sections in each chapter in the textbook. The answers to the **Multiple Choice Items**, **Completion Items**, and **Critical Thinking Exercises** are presented at the end of the **Chapter Test**.

Multiple Choice Items

Circle the letter that corresponds to the *best* alternative for each of the following items.

1. A critical distinction between learned behaviors and those that become possible through maturation, is that learned responses
   a. are innate, or preprogrammed.
   b. develop as a result of experience.
   c. outlast those that are gained through maturation.
   d. are acquired in strictly controlled laboratory conditions.

2. In classical conditioning, the sound of Pavlov's meat powder served as the
   a. unconditioned stimulus.
   b. conditioned stimulus.
   c. unconditioned response.
   d. conditioned response.

3. A student notices that his cat rushes into the kitchen as soon as the he opens a can of food with an electric can opener. In this example, the conditioned stimulus is the
   a. can of food.
   b. sound of the electric can opener.
   c. cat's food dish.
   d. cat rushing into the kitchen.

4. When people flinch when they see a long needle being stuck through a balloon, they are demonstrating
   a. spontaneous recovery.
   b. extinction.
   c. an unconditioned response.
   d. a conditioned response.

5. After a classically conditioned salivation response has been extinguished, dogs will occasionally salivate when the conditioned stimulus is presented without the meat powder. This behavior is an example of
   a. spontaneous recovery.
   b. extinction.
   c. an unconditioned response.
   d. a conditioned response.

6. After being frightened by a seagull who took a cracker from the child's hand, the child exhibits fear of all birds, even the family's pet canary. The child's behavior is an example of
   a. spontaneous recovery.
   b. extinction.
   c. generalization.
   d. discrimination.

7. After an interval, the child frightened by a seagull learns that not all birds are as aggressive as seagulls, so the child does not exhibit fear of all birds, including the family's pet canary. The child's new behavior is an example of
    a. spontaneous recovery.
    b. extinction.
    c. generalization.
    d. discrimination.

8. An application of classical conditioning in everyday life is
    a. the acquisition of phobias.
    b. spontaneous recovery of lost memories.
    c. learning to ride a bicycle.
    d. elimination of inappropriate classroom behaviors.

9. A situation in which the conditionability of a CS is weakened when it is paired with a US that has previously been paired with another CS is
    a. blocking.
    b. contingency management.
    c. learning motives.
    d. latent learning.

10. After drinking too much orange-flavored vodka and becoming ill, a student who becomes ill when offered another drink flavored with oranges
    a. is demonstrating blocking.
    b. has developed a set of contingencies.
    c. has developed a taste aversion.
    d. is being negatively reinforced.

11. A student who earns bonus points for making an outstanding class presentation has received a
    a. positive reinforcer.
    b. negative reinforcer.
    c. learned motive.
    d. learned goal.

12. The student earning bonus points for making an outstanding class presentation is an example of
    a. classical conditioning.
    b. operant conditioning.
    c. latent learning.
    d. insight learning.

13. A student whose headache disappears when her roommate responds to her request to lower the volume on the TV has experienced a
    a. positive reinforcer.
    b. negative reinforcer.
    c. learned motive.
    d. learned goal.

14. An instructor who tries to motivate students by praising them when they do well is applying the principles of
    a. continuous reinforcement.
    b. insight learning.
    c. positive reinforcement.
    d. observational learning.

15. A student's increased studying behavior designed to stop her parents nagging about her failure to live up to her academic potential is an example of
    a. positive punishment.
    b. negative punishment.
    c. positive reinforcement.
    d. negative reinforcement.

16. An example of a primary reinforcer is
    a. money.
    b. poker chips.
    c. gold stars.
    d. food.

17. An example of a secondary reinforcer is
    a. money.
    b. water.
    c. sleep.
    d. food.

18. A secondary reinforcer
    a. always follows the CS in classical conditioning.
    b. concerns items of interest after basic needs have been met.
    c. can sometimes go unnoticed by the participant, but is nevertheless powerful.
    d. acquires reinforcing properties by virtue of an association with a primary reinforcer.

19. Shaping involves
    a. reinforcement of the target response.
    b. reinforcement of activity other than the target response.
    c. reinforcement that does not follow every target response.
    d. reinforcement of successive approximations of the target response.

20. A psychologists who recommends that a couple attempt to eliminate their child's tantrums by ignoring the child during tantrums is applying the principle of
    a. generalization.
    b. discrimination.
    c. extinction.
    d. punishment.

21. Knowing to stop when a traffic light is red and go when it is green is attributable to our ability to interpret a
    a. cumulative record of our behavior.
    b. discriminative stimulus.
    c. set of incentives.
    d. schedule of reinforcement.

22. A cumulative record is
    a. the peak response rate in a Skinner box.
    b. a way of displaying results of conditioning trials.
    c. another name for the acquisition strength of a trial.
    d. way to distinguish generalization and discrimination.

23. If a teenager is given an allowance of $15 every two weeks if he cleans his room and takes out the garbage on Monday nights, the positive reinforcement of $15 is being given on a
    a. fixed interval schedule.
    b. fixed ratio schedule.
    c. variable interval schedule.
    d. variable ratio schedule.

24. A student who is paid $10 for every 100 concert flyers he distributes is on a
    a. fixed interval schedule.
    b. fixed ratio schedule.
    c. variable interval schedule.
    d. variable ratio schedule.

25. Students who are given unannounced quizzes are on a
    a. fixed interval schedule.
    b. fixed ratio schedule.
    c. variable interval schedule.
    d. variable ratio schedule.

26. The partial reinforcement effect
    a. results from administering only a portion of a reward each time.
    b. is powerful regardless of the quality of the reinforcer used.
    c. describes the pattern of responding when one responds only part of the time on an interval schedule.
    d. is demonstrated when extinction takes longer following intermittent reinforcement than after continuous reinforcement.

27. A parent administering punishment is attempting to
    a. increase the occurrence of a desirable behavior.
    b. decrease the occurrence of an undesirable behavior.
    c. increase the child's ability to discriminate desirable and undesirable behaviors.
    d. decrease the effect of insight learning of undesirable behaviors.

28. A student who suddenly sees the solution to a calculus problem after nearly an hour of study and a number of false starts is demonstrating
    a. insight learning.
    b. latent learning.
    c. generalization.
    d. discrimination.

29. A student who has lived in the town in which her university is located for two semesters is able to find store she has never visited before due to
    a. insight learning.
    b. latent learning.
    c. generalization.
    d. discrimination.

30. When younger siblings watch their older siblings be punished or reinforced for a specific behavior, the younger siblings experience
    a. behavior modification.
    b. observational learning.
    c. synthesis of vicarious activation.
    d. prolonged extinction trials for acquired responses.

Completion Items
Complete the following statements with key terms or concepts from the textbook.

1. Learning that occurs when a previously neutral stimulus and an unconditioned stimulus become associated is _____.

2. Reactions produced automatically when certain stimuli are presented are _____.

3. The appearance of an extinguished CR after some time has passed is _____.

4. A sprinter making a false start after hearing a car backfire is an example of _____.

5. A sprinter not making a false start after hearing a car backfire is an example of _____.
6. Motives acquired through the process of classical conditioning are _____.

7. Learned goals acquired the process of classical conditioning are also known as _____.

8. A person who becomes nauseated after eating an unfamiliar food, and then avoids that food in the future has experienced _____.

9. The process by which learning occurs when a participant makes a response that produces a change in the environment is _____.

10. Reinforcers promote learning and punishers lead to unlearning responses is a statement of the _____.

11. An event or stimulus that increases the frequency of the response it follows is a(n) _____.

12. A stimulus that has innate reinforcing properties is a(n) _____.

13. A preset pattern of delivering reinforcement is a(n) _____.

14. Reinforcement that follows every target response is _____.

15. Reinforcement that does not follow every target response is _____.

16. A reinforcement schedule in which reinforcement is based on the number of responses is a(n) _____ schedule.

17. A reinforcement schedule in which reinforcement is based on the passage of time is a(n) _____ schedule.

18. "Time out" is an example of a(n) _____.

19. Many teenagers know the laws regarding when to stop, and when to drive through intersections with traffic lights before taking driver education classes due to _____.

20. Arguments that video games are responsible for increased violence among teens and young adults is based on research on _____.

Critical Thinking Exercises

For the two case studies below, identify the appropriate learning terms associated with each case in the space provided.

1. As a young boy, a student was viciously attacked by a poodle, and he has been afraid of all dogs since that incident. As a result, he avoids dogs and even pictures of dogs. Last week, he turned a corner and saw a cocker spaniel, and his anxiety level increased. He ran as fast as he could and felt better after putting some distance between himself and the cocker spaniel.

What type of learning is occurring in this case study?

What are the significant stimuli and responses involved?

2. It is time for a young girl to learn how to tie her shoelaces. Her older sister takes her through it step-by-step. First, she is shown how to hold one lace in her hand and then the other lace. Then she learns to join the laces together. At each step, her sister praises her and gives her some apple juice. After about an hour, she can tie her shoelaces like a pro!

What type of learning is occurring in this case study?

What are the significant stimuli and responses involved?

Chapter Test Answers
Multiple Choice Items

1.b	11. a	21. b
2.a	12. b	22. b
3. b	13. b	23. a
4. d	14. c	24. b
5. a	15. d	25. c
6. c	16. d	26. d
7. d	17. a	27. b
8. a	18. d	28. a
9. a	19. d	29. b
10. c	20. c	30. b

Completion Items

1. classical conditioning	11. reinforcer
2. unconditioned responses	12. primary reinforcer
3. spontaneous recovery	13. schedule of reinforcement
4. generalization	14. continuous reinforcement
5. discrimination	15. intermittent (partial)reinforcement
6. learned motives	16. ratio
7. incentives	17. interval
8. taste-aversion learning	18. punisher
9. operant conditioning	19. latent learning
10.law of effect	20. observational learning (modeling)

Critical Thinking Exercises

1. Both classical and operant conditioning are occurring in the case study about the student's fear of dogs. The acquired his fear of dogs from his one experience with the poodle. He has generalized his anxiety and fear to all dogs. The poodle is the conditioned stimulus that was paired with the pain from the dog bite, the unconditioned stimulus. This pain produced fear and anxiety, which was the unconditioned response. He has generalized the conditioned response of anxiety to all dogs, not just poodles. To reduce his anxiety and fear, he runs away from dogs. By running away, he reduces his anxiety, which is an annoying stimulus to him. Therefore, the act of running away from dogs is not only a conditioned response, but it also serves as a negative reinforcer because running away reduces his anxiety.

2. The case study involving the young girl is using operant conditioning. She is learning to tie her shoes via shaping, a series of successive approximations to tying one's shoes. Her older sister is using the primary reinforcers, apple juice and praise, to reinforce her successive behaviors while she is learning to tie her shoes.

Key Vocabulary Terms: The terms listed in the margins of pages and entered in **boldface** type in the textbook are listed below with space for you to write the definitions. Remember that you may also want to create a list of the terms entered in italics in the textbook, especially those your instructor mentions in lectures. Again, you should try to write definitions *in your own words* because translating the terms into familiar language will facilitate retention.

learning

classical conditioning

neutral stimulus (NS)

unconditioned stimulus (US)

conditioned stimulus (CS)

unconditioned response (UR)

conditioned response (CR)

spontaneous recovery

generalization

discrimination

phobia

learned motives

learned goals (incentives)

blocking

taste-aversion learning

operant conditioning

law of effect

reinforcer

positive reinforcer

negative reinforcer

positive reinforcement

negative reinforcement

primary reinforcer

secondary reinforcer

shaping

extinction

discriminative stimulus

cumulative record

schedule of reinforcement

continuous reinforcement

intermittent (partial) reinforcement

ratio schedule

interval schedule

partial reinforcement effect

punisher

punishment

insight learning

latent learning

observational learning (modeling)

CHAPTER 6

Motivation and Emotion

Notes from Class and the Textbook

Use the space provided in this outline to record notes from the textbook as well as from class lectures and discussion.

I. What is Motivation?

II. Theories of Motivation

    A. Biological Theories

        1. Ethology

        2. Internal States, Drives, and Drive Reduction

        3. Optimum-Level Theories

Consider the *Psychological Detective* activity on p. 214 in the textbook.

    B. Cognitive Theories

        1. Cognitive-Consistency Theories

        2. Incentive Theories

        3. Maslow's Hierarchy of Needs

Consider the *Study Tip* on p. 216 in the textbook.

        4. Motives and Conflict

III. Specific Motives

    A. Hunger

        1. Nutrition and Eating

        2. How Does My Weight Compare?

Consider the *Psychological Detective* activity on p. 221 in the textbook.

        3. The Body Mass Index (BMI)

        4. The Biology of Obesity

        5. Social Factors and Cultural Factors in Weight

        6. Dieting

        7. Eating Disorders

    B. Sex

1. External Factors

Consider the *Psychological Detective* activity on p. 227 in the textbook.

2. Hormones

3. Brain Mechanisms

4. The Sexual Response

C. Achievement

Consider the *Study Tip* on p. 231 in the textbook.

IV. The What and the Why of Emotion

A. Relating Emotions and Behavior: The Evolutionary Perspective

V. The Physiological Components of Emotions

A. Early Theories of Emotions

1. The James-Lange Theory

2. The Cannon-Bard Theory

Consider the *Study Tip* on p. 236 in the textbook.

    B.   Physiological Differences among Emotions

    C.   The Role of the Brain in Emotion

Consider the *Psychological Detective* activity on p. 238 in the textbook.

        1. The Brain's Hemispheres and Emotions

        2. Lack of Emotion

    D. Evaluating the Lie Detector

Consider the *Psychological Detective* activity on p. 241 in the textbook.

VI. The Expressive Components of Emotions

A. Universal Elements in the Facial Expression of Emotion

   1. How Many Emotions Are There?

Consider the *Study Tip* on p. 246 in the textbook.

   2. The Facial Feedback Hypothesis

Consider the *Psychological Detective* activity on pp. 246-247 in the textbook.

   3. Display Rules: The Effects of Culture

   4. Smiling

Consider the *Psychological Detective* activity on p. 248 in the textbook.

B. Nonverbal Communication

   1. Body Language

   2. Paralanguage

Chapter Test

In addition to completing the practice items that follow, remember to complete the items in the *Check Your Progress* sections in each chapter in the textbook. The answers to the **Multiple Choice Items**, **Completion Items**, and **Critical Thinking Exercises** are presented at the end of the **Chapter Test**.

Multiple Choice Items

Circle the letter that corresponds to the *best* alternative for each of the following items.

1. Instincts are
    a. essentially reflexes.
    b. earned species-specific behaviors.
    c. internal representations of physiological needs.
    d. unlearned behaviors that are more complex than reflexes.

2. Drives are
    a. essentially reflexes.
    b. earned species-specific behaviors.
    c. internal representations of physiological needs.
    d. unlearned behaviors that are more complex than reflexes.

3. Drive reduction theory views motivated behavior as directed toward
    a. reducing physiological needs.
    b. increasing the possibility of attaining self-actualization.
    c. reducing negative psychophysical states.
    d. modifying attitudes that limit personal achievement.

4. The theory of motivation that would explain why people who move out of cities to get some "peace and quiet" move back because the country is "too quiet" is
    a. drive-reduction theory.
    b. incentive theory.
    c. optimum-level theory.
    d. cognitive theory.

5. The theories of motivation based on the processing and understanding of information are the
    a. drive-reduction theories.
    b. incentive theories.
    c. optimum-level theories.
    d. cognitive theories.

6. A person having inconsistent or incompatible thoughts or cognitions is experiencing
    a. emotional confusion.
    b. less than optimal arousal.
    c. cognitive dissonance.
    d. negative incentives.

7. The theory of motivation used by a third grade teacher who is trying to increase her students' exposure to books and reading by allowing the children to post a star sticker beside their names for each book they read is
    a. incentive theory.
    b. evolutionary theory.
    c. drive-reduction theory.
    d. optimum-level theory.

8. A person at the lowest level of Maslow's hierarchy of needs
    a. wants recognition for a recent promotion.
    b. is looking forward to spending holidays with family.
    c. is concerned about living in a high crime area.
    d. wonders whether there is any food at home.

9. A person at the level of Maslow's hierarchy of needs just below self-actualization
    a. wants recognition for a recent promotion.
    b. is looking forward to spending holidays with family.
    c. is concerned about living in a high crime area.
    d. wonders whether there is any food at home.

10. Self-actualization as conceptualized by Maslow is
    a. met concurrently with basic needs.
    b. reached by most people by the time they are 30.
    c. achieved by developing one's unique potential.
    d. an instinct and part of normal developmental processes.

11. A person who wants to learn to ski to be part of a group of friends who take numerous ski trips, but who hesitates due to the risk of injury is in
    a. an approach-approach conflict.
    b. an avoidance-avoidance conflict.
    c. an approach-avoidance conflict.
    d. a multiple approach-avoidance conflict.

12. The percentage of body in excess of desirable body weight that defines obesity is
    a. 10%.
    b. 15%.
    c. 20%.
    d. 25%.

13. As a rule, people are considered obese if their BMI is
    a. ≥ 20.
    b. ≥ 30.
    c. ≥ 40.
    d. ≥ 50.

14. A characteristic belief of women who develop anorexia nervosa is
    a. a strong belief that they are fat.
    b. that BMI is a more important indicator of health than weight.
    c. a belief that controlling weight is potentially dangerous.
    d. minor weight gains are acceptable as long as weight loss follows quickly.

15. The most accurate description of bulimia nervosa would be
    a. self-starvation.
    b. gorging and purging.
    c. fear of becoming fat.
    d. fad dieting.

16. Animals communicate sexually through
    a. aphrodisiacs.
    b. androgens.
    c. estrogens.
    d. pheromones.

17. Following surgical removal the testes, the level of sexual interest will most likely
    a. increase.
    b. decrease.
    c. remain the same.
    d. disappear.

18. The category of specific motives most difficult to define precisely is
    a. sex.
    b. hunger.
    c. affiliation.
    d. achievement.

19. The James-Lange theory of emotion states that
    a. emotion precedes and causes bodily change.
    b. physiological changes precede emotion.
    c. only activity of the thalamus is involved in emotion.
    d. only the frontal lobes are involved in emotion.

20. The commonsense theory of emotion states that
    a. emotion precedes and causes bodily change.
    b. physiological changes precede emotion.
    c. only activity of the thalamus is involved in emotion.
    d. only the frontal lobes are involved in emotion.

21. The Cannon-Bard theory of emotion states that
    a. emotion precedes and causes bodily change.
    b. emotion and physiological changes occur simultaneously.
    c. only activity of the thalamus is involved in emotion.
    d. only the frontal lobes are involved in emotion.

22. The part of the brain that is most important when considering emotion is the
    a. cerebral cortex.
    b. reticular activation system.
    c. midbrain.
    d. limbic system.

23. Research involving showing pictures of people expressing a variety of emotions to people from all over the world has shown that
    a. there are four basic emotions.
    b. the number of emotions one may experience varies by culture.
    c. although emotions may be common across cultures, their expression varies widely.
    d. there is a high degree of agreement across cultures in recognizing basic emotions.

24. Across cultures, agreement is highest for facial expressions of
    a. disgust.
    b. fear.
    c. happiness.
    d. surprise.

25. A man reared to believe that men should not cry in public except at an immediate relative's funeral, and who does not cry except in this situation is following
    a. display rules.
    b. emblems.
    c. regulators.
    d. stereotypes.

26. Nodding to indicate agreement is an example of
    a. an adaptor.
    b. a regulator.
    c. an illustrator.
    d. an emblem.

27. A Russian premier who took off his shoe and pounded the podium for emphasis during a speech was using
    a. an adaptor.
    b. a regulator.
    c. an illustrator.
    d. an emblem.

28. A student observed doodling during a boring lecture is using
    a. an adaptor.
    b. a regulator.
    c. an illustrator.
    d. an emblem.

29. A student making a presentation in class whose rapid speech is an expression of anxiety is demonstrating
    a. a display rule.
    b. paralanguage.
    c. drive-reduction theory.
    d. achievement motivation.

30. Men are more likely than women to express the emotion of
    a. disgust.
    b. fear.
    c. surprise.
    d. anger.

Completion Items
Complete the following statements with key terms or concepts from the textbook.

1. The physiological and psychological factors that account for the arousal, direction, and persistence of behavior account for _____.

2. Behaviors triggered or released by specific environmental events called releasing stimuli are _____.

3. An internal motivational state created by a physiological need is a(n) _____.

4. The theory of motivation based on the idea that different people function better at different levels of arousal is _____ theory.

5. The highest level of Maslow's hierarchy of needs is _____.

6. The ratio of weight to height squared is the _____.

7. The minimum amount of energy required to keep an awake, resting body alive is the _____.

8. A man who weighs less than 85% of his expected weight and whose testosterone levels are low most likely has _____.

9. A person who develops medical problems as a result of overuse of laxatives most likely has _____.

10. The menstrual synchrony found among lesbian couples has supported speculation about the role of _____ in controlling some aspects of human behavior.

11. A psychologist administering the Thematic Apperception Test to a client is assessing _____ motivation.

12. Research on the universality of emotions has demonstrated that there are at least _____ emotions that are recognized everywhere.

13. The theory that physiological responses precede and cause emotions is the _____ theory.

14. The theory that emotional feelings and physiological responses of emotion occur simultaneously is the _____ theory.

15. The instrument that uses physiological responses to detect lying is a(n) _____.

16. A person who smiles at an angry person in order to defuse an uncomfortable situation is applying the _____.

17. Cultural norms that tell one to laugh when someone tells a joke are _____.

18. A person who decides that another person is being sincere because the person is making direct eye contact is interpreting _____.

19. The most common nonverbal regulator is the _____.

20. Communication that involves aspects of speech such as how fast one speaks and tone of voice is _____.

Critical Thinking Exercises

Statement	Identify the Associated Theory
I think that behavior is motivated by a desire to reduce the internal tension caused by my unmet biological needs. My needs <u>push</u> me to behave in certain ways.	
I think that people are motivated, psychologically and cognitively, to "be all that they can be": to realize their potential.	
I think that evolution has wired our brains to engage in certain behaviors, like mating and reproducing, to ensure that our genes make it into the next generation.	
I think that my behavior is shaped by a need for stimulation. When I am bored I try to increase my arousal by increasing the level of stimulation in my environment.	
I think that my behavior and yours is shaped by a system of rewards like money, love, and recognition.	

Chapter Test Answers
Multiple Choice Items

1. d	11. c	21. b
2. c	12. c	22. d
3. a	13. b	23. d
4. c	14. a	24. c
5. d	15. b	25. a
6. c	16. d	26. d
7. a	17. b	27. c
8. d	18. d	28. a
9. a	19. b	29. b
10. c	20. a	30. d

Completion Items

1. motivation	11. achievement
2. instincts	12. sex
3. drive	13. James-Lange
4. optimum-level	14. Cannon-Bard
5. self-actualization	15. polygraph
6. body mass index	16. facial feedback hypothesis
7. basal metabolism rate	17. display rules
8. anorexia nervosa	18. nonverbal communication
9. bulimia nervosa	19. handshake
10. pheromones	20. paralanguage

Critical Thinking Exercises

Statement	Identify the Associated Cognitive Theory
I think that behavior is motivated by a desire to reduce the internal tension caused by my unmet biological needs. My needs <u>push</u> me to behave in certain ways.	Internal States, Drives and Drive Reduction
I think that people are motivated, psychologically and cognitively, to "be all that they can be": to realize their potential.	Maslow's Hierarchy of Needs
I think that evolution has wired our brains to engage in certain behaviors, like mating and reproducing, to ensure that our genes make it into the next generation.	Ethology
I think that my behavior is shaped by a need for stimulation. When I am bored I try to increase my arousal by increasing the level of stimulation in my environment.	Optimum-Level
I think that my behavior and yours is shaped by a system of rewards like money, love, and recognition.	Incentive Theory

Key Vocabulary Terms: The terms listed in the margins of pages and entered in **boldface** type in the textbook are listed below with space for you to write the definitions. Remember that you may also want to create a list of the terms entered in italics in the textbook, especially those your instructor mentions in lectures. Again, you should try to write definitions *in your own words* because translating the terms into familiar language will facilitate retention.

motivation

instincts

drive

drive-reduction theory

optimum-level theory

cognitive dissonance

hierarchy of needs

self-actualization

obesity

body mass index (BMI)

anorexia nervosa

bulimia nervosa

pheromones

achievement

emotion

James-Lange theory

commonsense view of emotion

Cannon-Bard theory

polygraph

facial feedback hypothesis

display rules

nonverbal communication

paralanguage

CHAPTER 7

Memory

Notes from Class and the Textbook
Use the space provided in this outline to record notes from the textbook as well as from class lectures and discussion.

I. Initial Studies

Consider the *Psychological Detective* activity on p. 260 in the textbook.

    A. The Curve of Forgetting

    B. Recognition and Relearning

II. Models of Memory

    A. Human Memory as an Information Processing System

        1. Encoding

        2. Storage

        3. Retrieval

Consider the *Psychological Detective* activity on p. 264 in the textbook.

Complete the *Myth or Science* activity on p. 264 in the textbook.

Consider the *Study Tip* on p. 264 in the textbook.

    B. The Stages-of-Memory Model

        1.   Sensory Memory

Consider the *Psychological Detective* activity on p. 266 in the textbook.

        2.   Short-Term Memory

Consider the *Psychological Detective* activity on p. 267 in the textbook.

Consider the *Psychological Detective* activity on p. 267 in the textbook.

3. Long-Term Memory

4. Forgetting

III. Other Approaches to Learning and Memory

A. The Levels-of-Processing Model

Consider the *Study Tip* on p. 274 in the textbook.

B. Different Types of Long-Term Memory

1. Semantic Memory

Consider the *Psychological Detective* activity on p. 276 in the textbook.

Complete the *Hands On* activity on p. 276 in the textbook.

2. Episodic Memory

3. Priming

4. Procedural Memory

Consider the *Study Tip* on p. 279 in the textbook.

C. Retrieval

1. Retrieval from STM

Consider the *Psychological Detective* activity on p. 279 in the textbook.

2. Retrieval from LTM

3. Encoding Specificity

Consider the *Psychological Detective* activity on p. 281 in the textbook.

4. Eyewitness Testimony

5. State-Dependent Learning

D. The Repressed/Recovery Memory Controversy

E. Memory Illusions

IV. Techniques for Improving Memory

A. Influential Factors

B. Processing Strategies

1. Imagery

2. Method of Loci

Consider the *Psychological Detective* activity on p. 288 in the textbook.

3. Pegword Technique

4. Grouping (Chunking)

5. Coding

6. Acronyms and Acrostics

Consider the *Study Tip* on p. 290 in the textbook.

V. The Physiological Basis of Learning and Memory

    A. Amnesias

        1.   Anterograde Amnesia and the Hippocampus

Consider the *Psychological Detective* activity on p. 290 in the textbook.

        2.   Retrograde Amnesia and the Consolidation Hypothesis

Chapter Test

In addition to completing the practice items that follow, remember to complete the items in the *Check Your Progress* sections in each chapter in the textbook. The answers to the **Multiple Choice Items, Completion Items,** and **Critical Thinking Exercises** are presented at the end of the **Chapter Test**.

Multiple Choice Items

Circle the letter that corresponds to the *best* alternative for each of the following items.

1. Ebbinghaus used nonsense syllables in his studies of memory
    a.   because they were short.
    b.   because they were supposed to have no meaning.
    c.   to encourage cross-cultural replications of his studies.
    d.   because generating the consonant-vowel-consonant sequence was easy.

2. If participants in a memory study are asked to memorize and repeat lists of words in the order in which they were presented, the study involves a
  a. recognition procedure.
  b. free recall procedure.
  c. serial learning procedure.
  d. randomized recall procedure.

3. If participants in a memory study are asked to memorize and repeat lists of words in any order, the study involves a
  a. recognition procedure.
  b. free recall procedure.
  c. serial learning procedure.
  d. randomized recall procedure.

4. If a student studying the lists of Key Vocabulary Terms notices that she remembers the terms at the beginning and end of the lists better than the terms in the middle, the student's learning is being affected by
  a. the serial position effect.
  b. the method of loci.
  c. procedural memory.
  d. episodic memory.

5. If a psychologist measures the time required for students who took psychology in high school to learn familiar terms in the Key Vocabulary Terms, the instructor is measuring
  a. the difference score.
  b. proactive interference.
  c. working memory.
  d. the savings score.

6. The stage of the memory process in which information is transformed for storage is
  a. encoding.
  b. storage.
  c. retrieval.
  d. transferral.

7. The stage of the memory process in which information is brought into consciousness is
  a. encoding.
  b. storage.
  c. retrieval.
  d. transferral.

8. According to the Atkinson-Shiffrin model, sensory memories
  a. generally last about 20 seconds.
  b. may be remembered for a lifetime.
  c. tend to be very distracting.
  d. generally last 0.5 - 1 second.

9. According to the Atkinson-Shiffrin model, short-term memories
  a. generally last about 20 seconds.
  b. may be remembered for a lifetime.
  c. tend to be very distracting.
  d. generally last 0.5 - 1 second.

10. According to the Atkinson-Shiffrin model, a student responding to a multiple choice test item is using
    a. sensory memory.
    b. short-term memory.
    c. working memory.
    d. long-term memory..

11. If a student preparing for a test in a course that includes many new terms writes a sentence using each new term that has meaning based on the student's life, the student is using
    a. maintenance rehearsal.
    b. elaborative rehearsal.
    c. paired associate learning.
    d. serial learning.

12. If a student first studies psychology and then sociology, and then has difficulty remembering sociology terms on a sociology test, the student is experiencing
    a. long-term memory decay.
    b. negative transfer.
    c. proactive interference.
    d. retroactive interference.

13. If a student first studies psychology and then sociology, and then has difficulty remembering psychology terms on a psychology test, the student is experiencing
    a. long-term memory decay.
    b. negative transfer.
    c. proactive interference.
    d. retroactive interference.

14. The levels-of-processing theory states that
    a. as processing depth increases, probability of recall increases.
    b. as processing depth increases, probability of recall decreases.
    c. the probability of recall is independent of processing depth.
    d. the probability of recall expressed mathematically as one over the depth of processing.

15. Students' memories of where they were and what they were doing when they learned about the events of September 11, 2001 are
    a. eidetic imagery.
    b. a semantic network.
    c. explicit memories.
    d. implicit memories.

16. Remembering the three stages of memory in order to take a test including material covered in this chapter is an example of
    a. procedural memory.
    b. serial learning.
    c. episodic memory.
    d. semantic memory.

17. Memories of personal experiences, events and the setting in which they occurred are called
    a. procedural memories.
    b. semantic memories.
    c. short-term memories.
    d. episodic memories.

18. Students' memories of where they were and what they were doing when they learned about the events of September 11, 2001 can also be considered a
   a. flashbulb memory.
   b. relearning test.
   c. schema.
   d. priming memory.

19. The type of memory that operates at an unconscious level is
   a. eidetic imagery.
   b. priming memory.
   c. episodic memory.
   d. short-term memory.

20. Even if a student has not ridden a bicycle in years, the fact that the student can still ride one is evidence that the student has
   a. long-term memory.
   b. episodic memory.
   c. priming memory.
   d. procedural memory.

21. A network of related concepts that are linked together is a
   a. schema.
   b. semantic network.
   c. flashbulb memory.
   d. nondeclarative memory.

22. A student seeing a dentist for a six-month checkup is surprised that X-rays are to be taken and asks about the X-rays taken on her previous visit. If no X-rays were taken during the previous visit, the type of memory would explain the student's "memory" of having had X-rays is
   a. eidetic imagery of dental checkups.
   b. proactive interference from earlier dental checkups.
   c. chunking information into LTM about dental checkups.
   d. a schema based on earlier dental visits.

23. A psychology instructor who advises a student who is not doing well in the course to study in the classroom whenever possible is applying the principle of
   a. encoding specificity.
   b. maintenance rehearsal.
   c. semantic networking.
   d. level-of-processing.

24. The student who is not doing well in the psychology course could also
   a. reduce the number of study sessions.
   b. use distributed study sessions.
   c. group dissimilar concepts and terms for study sessions.
   d. apply the concept of maintenance rehearsal.

25. The phrase "Roy G. Biv" used as a technique for remembering the colors of the electromagnetic spectrum is an example of
   a. semantic memory..
   b. priming memory.
   c. a schema.
   d. a mnemonic device.

26. If a person has five items on a grocery list and associates each item with a specific place between the person's house and the grocery store, the person is using
    a. the method of loci.
    b. an acronym.
    c. an acrostic.
    d. the pegword method.

27. The phrase "Roy G. Biv" used as a technique for remembering the colors of the electromagnetic spectrum is also an example of
    a. the method of loci.
    b. an acronym.
    c. an acrostic.
    d. the pegword method.

28. The memory aid consisting of a verse in which the first letters of each line stands for a bit of information is
    a. the method of loci.
    b. an acronym.
    c. an acrostic.
    d. the pegword method.

29. If a person is resuscitated after several minutes of not breathing following a heart attack and is then unable to store new memories, the person is experiencing
    a. paramnesia.
    b. cryptoamnesia.
    c. anterograde amnesia.
    d. retrograde amnesia.

30. If a person has no memory of events prior to suffering a severe head injury in an automobile wreck, the person is experiencing
    a. paramnesia.
    b. cryptoamnesia.
    c. anterograde amnesia.
    d. retrograde amnesia.

Completion Items
Complete the following statements with key terms or concepts from the textbook.

1. Students learning vocabulary for a foreign language often use _____ learning.

2. A multiple choice item is an example of a _____ test.

3. A psychologist interested in how quickly students volunteering to work as translators at a local hospital, but who have not spoken Spanish since high school, can become conversational again, would conduct a _____ test.

4. Information cannot be retrieved for a test unless it is first _____.

5. The common term for eidetic imagery is _____.

6. When a student is using memory, attention and conscious effort are brought to bear in _____ memory.

7. Cramming for a test is a form of _____.

8. A student who keeps substituting words from her high school Spanish course in her tests in her college French course is experiencing _____.

9. The finding that people do better recalling words from a list when instructed to rate the pleasantness of each word as opposed to counting the number of letters in each word is evidence for the _____.

10. A student reciting the alphabet to remember another student's name is experiencing the _____.

11. Psychologists refer to memory of one's personal experiences as _____ memory.

12. Since it is unconscious memory processing, priming memory is a form of _____ memory.

13. After not playing volleyball since high school, a student quickly becomes the best player on her intramural team because of her _____.

14. People do not always know whether to tip wait staff at pizza restaurants because the context does not exactly match their _____ for either a fast-food restaurant or a restaurant.

15. Students who drink coffee when studying and make sure they have enough time to get a cup of coffee before taking a test are applying the concept of _____.

16. The special form of plagiarism in which students forget the original source of information and use it as if it were their own is _____.

17. A student who establishes a connection between a list of comic book superheroes and a list of psychological terms to be learned for a test is using the _____.

18. Music students who learned the phrase "Every Good Boy Does Fine" remember the five main notes in the treble clef were using a(n) _____.

19. Loss of memory following physical or psychological trauma is _____.

20. The hypothesis that memories must be set before they can be stored is the _____ hypothesis.

Critical Thinking Exercises

Can you trust an eyewitness?
1. Eyewitnesses to crimes are not always reliable. They think they remember details of the event, yet they make errors. Describe three psychological factors that might account for such errors in eyewitness testimony.

2. People are all eyewitnesses to their own lives, but they are not completely accurate in what they remember about their lives. Can you identify autobiographical memories that you think might be distorted or inaccurate and list the reasons why they may be inaccurate?

Chapter Test Answers
Multiple Choice Items

1. b	11. b	21. b
2. c	12. c	22. d
3. b	13. d	23. a
4. a	14. a	24. b
5. d	15. c	25. d
6. a	16. d	26. a
7. c	17. d	27. b
8. d	18. a	28. c
9. a	19. b	29. c
10. c	20. d	30. d

Completion Items

1. paired-associate	11. episodic
2. recognition	12. implicit
3. relearning	13. procedural memory
4. encoded	14. schema
5. photographic memory	15. state-dependent learning
6. working	16. cryptoamnesia
7. maintenance rehearsal	17. pegword technique
8. proactive interference	18. acronym
9. levels-of-processing model	19. amnesia
10. tip-of-the tongue phenomenon	20. consolidation

Critical Thinking Exercises

1. Witnesses to crimes have difficulty identifying differences between people of different races. They also tend to have a bias in that people are able to recall facial details of individuals of the same race. Research also shows that when a crime involves violence, people tend to recall fewer details than if violence was not involved. When people are being robbed at gunpoint, they generally tend to remember the gun because that is where they are looking, and not remember details of the person holding the gun. The third factor that can influence an eyewitness's account is the questions used to elicit information from the witness. Research by Loftus and colleagues has shown that altering the wording in a question can alter the memory of an eyewitness.

2. Many people have numerous inaccurate childhood memories. For example, people may remember falling down stairs and being hurt when the event never occurred. Instead, the event may have been "implanted" by a parent who frequently warned the person that he or she could be badly hurt by not being careful and falling down the stairs. Clearly, memories can be altered by suggestions from others, by talking about events and having others incorporate elements that never happened, and by normal forgetting.

Key Vocabulary Terms: The terms listed in the margins of pages and entered in **boldface** type in the textbook are listed below with space for you to write the definitions. Remember that you may also want to create a list of the terms entered in italics in the textbook, especially those your instructor mentions in lectures. Again, you should try to write definitions *in your own words* because translating the terms into familiar language will facilitate retention.

memory

nonsense syllables

serial learning

free recall

serial position effect

paired-associate learning

recognition test

relearning test

savings score

encoding

storage

retrieval

eidetic imagery

sensory memory

short-term memory (STM)

working memory

long-term memory (LTM)

maintenance rehearsal

elaborative rehearsal

proactive interference

retroactive interference

levels-of-processing model

explicit (or declarative)memory

implicit (or nondeclarative) memory

semantic memory

tip-of-the-tongue (TOT) phenomenon

episodic memory

flashbulb memory

priming or implicit memory

procedural memory

semantic network

schema

encoding specificity

state-dependent learning

mnemonic devices

method of loci

pegword technique

acronym

acrostic

amnesia

anterograde amnesia

retrograde amnesia

consolidation hypothesis

CHAPTER 8

Thinking, Language, and Intelligence

Notes from Class and the Textbook

Use the space provided in this outline to record notes from the textbook as well as from class lectures and discussion.

I. Thinking

    A. Cognitive Psychology

        1. Images

Consider the *Psychological Detective* activity on p.296 in the textbook.

        2. Concepts

Consider the *Psychological Detective* activity on p.297 in the textbook.

    B. Problem Solving

        1. Problem-Solving Methods

        2. Algorithms

Consider the *Psychological Detective* activity on p.299 in the textbook.

3. Heuristics

4. Obstacles and Aids to Problem Solving

5. Setting Subgoals

Consider the *Psychological Detective* activity on p.300 in the textbook.

6. Rigidity

Consider the *Psychological Detective* activity on p.301 in the textbook.

7. Set Effect

Consider the *Study Tip* on p.302 in the textbook.

C. Making Decisions

1. Seeking Information to Confirm a Solution

2. Representativeness

Consider the *Psychological Detective* activity on p.304 in the textbook.

3. Availability

4. Comparison

5. Framing

Consider the *Study Tip* on p.306 in the textbook.

D. Creativity

1. Defining Creativity

2. Measuring Creativity

3. Personal Factors in Creativity

4. Situational Factors in Creativity

5. Enhancing Creativity at Work

II. Language

    A. Language and Development

        1. The Acquisition of Language

        2. American Sign Language

    B. Thinking and Language

        1. Using Language to Limit Thought

        2. Language and Gender

Consider the *Psychological Detective* activity on p.317 in the textbook.

III. Intelligence

Consider the *Psychological Detective* activity on p.319 in the textbook.

    A. Cultural Views of Intelligence

B. The History of Intelligence Testing

   1. The Stanford-Binet Intelligence Scale

   2. The Wechsler Scales

Consider the *Study Tip* on p.322 in the textbook.

C. Principles of Psychological Tests

   1. Reliability

   2. Validity

   3. Standardization

D. Extremes of Intelligence

   1. Exceptional Children

   2. Savant Syndrome

E. Kinds of Intelligence

   1. Spearman's Model

   2. Sternberg's Mode

   3. Gardner's Multiple Intelligences

Consider the *Study Tip* on p.331 in the textbook.

    F. Misuse of Intelligence Tests

    G. Hereditary and Environmental Determinants of Intelligence

       1. Hereditary Determinants

Consider the *Psychological Detective* activity on p.332 in the textbook.

       2. Environmental Determinants of Intelligence

Complete the *Myth or Science* activity on p. 334 in the textbook.

Consider the *Psychological Detective* activity on p.335 in the textbook.

       3. Explaining Differences in Intelligence Scores

IV. Artificial Intelligence

    A. History

    B. Current Approaches to AI

        1. Top-Down/Symbolic AI

        2. Bottom-Up/Subsymbolic AI

    C. Critiquing AI

        1. The Turing Test

        2. Beyond the Turing Test

Chapter Test

In addition to completing the practice items that follow, remember to complete the items in the *Check Your Progress* sections in each chapter in the textbook. The answers to the **Multiple Choice Items**, **Completion Items**, and **Critical Thinking Exercises** are presented at the end of the **Chapter Test**.

Multiple Choice Items

Circle the letter that corresponds to the *best* alternative for each of the following items.

1. Manipulating information in the form of mental images or concepts is
    a.   creativity.
    b.   framing.
    c.   intelligence.
    d.   thinking.

2. If a two-year-old has a mental image of the family boxer every time she hears the word "dog," the family pet is the child's
    a.   algorithm for thinking about dogs.
    b.   prototype for the concept of dog.
    c.   frame for the word "dog."
    d.   availability heuristic for dog.

3. A student trying to solve a problem by systematically evaluating all possible solutions until the correct one is found is using
    a. an algorithm.
    b. the availability heuristic.
    c. a trial-and-error procedure.
    d. the representativeness heuristic.

4. The familiar spelling rule, 'i before e except after c,' is an example of
    a. an algorithm.
    b. a heuristic.
    c. a concept.
    d. a prototype.

5. A student who used a dime to open the battery bank on his camera overcame
    a. set effect.
    b. poor framing.
    c. confirmation bias.
    d. functional fixedness.

6. A frustrated statistics student complaining to an instructor that he cannot understand why the previous methods of interpreting results is not working is experiencing
    a. set effect.
    b. poor framing.
    c. confirmation bias.
    d. functional fixedness.

7. A student who states that the next number in the sequence 2, 4, 8, is 14 without considering the possibility that it is16 is demonstrating
    a. set effect.
    b. poor framing.
    c. confirmation bias.
    d. functional fixedness.

8. The gambler's fallacy is an example of
    a. confirmation bias.
    b. the representativeness heuristic.
    c. the availability heuristic.
    d. functional fixedness.

9. Although sanitation ratings are accurate predictors of the risk of becoming ill eating at restaurants with different ratings, if a well-publicized case of food poisoning at an expensive restaurant with a high sanitation rating makes a person decide to avoid restaurants with that rating, the person is applying the
    a. confirmation bias.
    b. the representativeness heuristic.
    c. the availability heuristic.
    d. functional fixedness.

10. Despite a weather forecast predicting a 70% chance of rain, a child who is trying to convince her father to take her to a theme park the next day, reports that there is a 30% chance of sunshine for tomorrow. The child is
    a. ignoring the possibility that her father understands confirmation bias.
    b. trying to convince her father that functional fixedness does not apply.
    c. manipulating the framing of her information about the weather report.
    d. hoping he will use the representativeness heuristic.

11. A student who notes that, in addition to looking up phone numbers, pages in a phone book can be used to start a fire when most of the other students are noting that a phone book can be used as a booster seat, is demonstrating
    a. creativity.
    b. good framing.
    c. savant syndrome.
    d. functional fixedness.

12. A psychologist conducting a study of the personality characteristics of creative people would find that they are
    a. willing to take risks.
    b. lazy.
    c. have little tolerance for ambiguity.
    d. very neat.

13. While defining creativity is difficult, one characteristic is ability to use
    a. random thinking.
    b. divergent thinking.
    c. emergent thinking.
    d. convergent thinking.

14. When an infant utters "ma, ma, ma. ma." the sound is a
    a. cognition.
    b. phoneme.
    c. morpheme.
    d. syntax fragment.

15. When an infant utters "mama, mama." the sound is a
    a. cognition.
    b. phoneme.
    c. morpheme.
    d. syntax fragment.

16. A woman whose first language is not English visiting the United States notices that all evidence of an overnight snowfall has disappeared by mid morning and says "Always here it does not snow properly," demonstrating that she has not mastered English language
    a. pronunciation.
    b. morphemes.
    c. phonemes.
    d. syntax.

17. Double speak is intended to
    a. make good seem bad.
    b. turn positives into negatives.
    c. make nonstandard language acceptable.
    d. shift or avoid responsibility.

18. To account for age-related differences in ability levels, Binet and Simon proposed the concept of
    a. heritability.
    b. mental age.
    c. intelligence.
    d. chronological age.

19. Binet and Simon calculated the intelligence quotient using the formula
   a. MA/CA*100.
   b. CA/MA*100.
   c. (CA*100)/MA.
   d. (MA*100)/CA.

20. A person who completed a depression inventory six months ago and again yesterday had similar scores at each testing suggests that the person was experiencing high levels of depression, indicating that the inventory appears to
   a. be standardized.
   b. have high reliability.
   c. have low validity.
   d. acceptable norms.

21. A person who completed a depression inventory six months ago and again yesterday had similar scores at each testing and that indicated high levels of depression; however, the person has had no symptoms of depression and, in fact, scores on other established depression inventories suggest that he is not depressed, indicating that the depression inventory appears to
   a. be standardized.
   b. have high reliability.
   c. have low validity.
   d. acceptable norms.

22. The development specific instructions for administering a test and the determination of appropriate time limits for the test are aspects of establishing
   a. reliability.
   b. validity.
   c. norms.
   d. standardization.

23. The purpose of administering a test to obtain scores from a large sample is necessary to establish
   a. reliability.
   b. validity.
   c. norms.
   d. standardization.

24. A characteristic of the normal curve is that it is
   a. rarely observed with biological and psychological variables.
   b. asymmetrical with 2/3 of the scores above the mean and 1/3 below the mean.
   c. a bell-shaped distribution of scores with the majority clustered in the middle.
   d. produced when there is a strong, positive relationship between two variables.

25. A person with an IQ between 50 and 70 is said to have
   a. mild mental retardation.
   b. moderate mental retardation.
   c. severe mental retardation.
   d. profound mental retardation.

26. A person with an IQ below 20 is said to have
   a. mild mental retardation.
   b. moderate mental retardation.
   c. severe mental retardation.
   d. profound mental retardation.

27. A person with the savant syndrome would have
    a. a learning disability.
    b. one remarkable ability.
    c. a variety of artistic abilities.
    d. a high level of creativity.

28. A student who has experienced significant difficulty with the acquisition and use of reading abilities has
    a. mild mental retardation.
    b. savant syndrome.
    c. superlative skills in other areas.
    d. a learning disability.

29. The proportion of intelligence that is attributable to genetics is called the
    a. biology of intelligence.
    b. heredity of intelligence.
    c. chemistry of intelligence.
    d. heritability of intelligence.

30. If environmental variables are the key determinants of intelligence, the pair of people who would have the most similar intelligence scores would be
    a. fraternal twins reared apart.
    b. identical twins reared apart.
    c. adoptive siblings reared together.
    d. adoptive siblings adopted after each was six years old.

Completion Items
Complete the following statements with key terms or concepts from the textbook.

1. Mental categories that share common characteristics are _____.

2. The most typical example of a particular concept is a(n) _____.

3. A student who wants to apply a method that is certain to solve a problem will apply a(n) _____.

4. Educated guesses or rules of thumb that may solve a problem are _____.

5. An elementary school student who persists in trying to solve an arithmetic problem using a multiplication process that had worked previously when division is required is demonstrating the _____.

6. The heuristic by which a person makes a decision based on whether an object, person, or event resembles a prototype is the _____ heuristic.

7. The tendency for decision making to be based on the influence of positive or negative outcomes is _____.

8. The smallest unit of sound in language is a(n) _____.

9. The smallest unit of meaning in language is a(n) _____.

10. The ability to excel at a variety of tasks, especially academic tasks is _____.
11. The question of whether a test measures what it measures consistently is answered by _____.

12. The question of whether a test measures what it is intended to measure is answered by _____.

13. The procedures for administering the SAT test are the same no matter where the test is given because the test has undergone _____.

14. The percentiles available to compare student scores on the SAT are an example of _____.

15. The curve characteristic of many variables in biological and psychological variables is the _____ curve.

16. The triarchic theory of intelligence is proposed by _____.

17. A model of intelligence based multiple intelligences is proposed by _____.

18. If a psychologist calculates that 40% of the differences between two groups in intelligence is due to inherited factors, the psychologist has calculated the _____.

19. Twins who are no more related than other siblings are _____ twins.

20. The development of machines capable of engaging intelligent processes is _____.

Critical Thinking Exercises

1. After a meeting with a school psychologist, a mother is quite upset because she has been told that her son's IQ scores fall in the average range. The mother is sure that her son is not "just average" because he has been earning A's in elementary school. How can information presented in this chapter help the mother gain a better understanding of what her child's test scores indicate?

2. A man has been planning a trip to another state to visit his younger sister for four months, buying his plane tickets three months ago. Last night, a plane crashed in another country killing 150 people. The man is now arranging to rent a car to drive nearly a thousand miles to visit his sister because he now believes that planes are unsafe. What decision-making strategy has the man employed?

Chapter Test Answers
Multiple Choice Items

1. d	11. a	21. c
2. b	12. a	22. d
3. a	13. b	23. c
4. b	14. b	24. c
5. d	15. c	25. a
6. a	16. d	26. d
7. c	17. d	27. b
8. b	18. b	28. d
9. c	19. a	29. d
10. c	20. b	30. b

Completion Items

1. concepts	11. reliability
2. nprototype	12. validity
3. algorithm	13. standardization
4. heuristics	14. norms
5. set effect	15. normal
6. representativeness	16. Sternberg
7. framing	17. Gardner
8. phoneme	18. heritability
9. morpheme	19. fraternal
10. intelligence	20. artificial intelligence

Critical Thinking Exercises

1. Most people like to think that they have above average intelligence. Intelligence scores tend to follow a normal, or bell-shaped, curve and most people fall in the highest part of the distribution (or bell), which is the "average range." The mother should also be aware that not even the experts agree when defining intelligence. Some psychologists believe there are multiple forms of intelligence, some three different kinds, and still others a general factor called *g*. Her son's grades in school actually reflect what he has learned, which is achievement, and, while intelligence is often related to achievement, that is not always the case. Some very intelligent students never study enough to make high grades. Most experts agree that intelligence involves the ability to think abstractly, acquire knowledge, and solve problems, and most IQ tests do a fair job of measuring those skills. However, skills like creativity, motivation, goal-directed behavior, and a willingness to work hard are not captured by traditional intelligence tests, but these skills tend to be good predictors of success in the life.

2. The man has employed the availability heuristic, a strategy in which the likelihood of an event is estimated on the basis of how readily available other instances of the event are in memory. The man would actually be much safer flying than driving.

Key Vocabulary Terms: The terms listed in the margins of pages and entered in **boldface** type in the textbook are listed below with space for you to write the definitions. Remember that you may also want to create a list of the terms entered in italics in the textbook, especially those your instructor mentions in lectures. Again, you should try to write definitions *in your own words* because translating the terms into familiar language will facilitate retention.

cognitive psychology

thinking

concepts

prototype

algorithm

heuristics

functional fixedness

set effect

confirmation bias

representativeness heuristic

availability heuristic

framing

creativity

phoneme

morpheme

syntax

mental age

intelligence quotient (IQ)

intelligence

reliability

validity

standardization

norms

normal curve

savant syndrome

heritability

identical twins

fraternal twins

artificial intelligence (AI)

CHAPTER 9

Development Across the Lifespan

Notes from Class and the Textbook

Use the space provided in this outline to record notes from the textbook as well as from class lectures and discussion.

I. Basic Issues in Developmental Psychology

    A. Nature and Nurture

Consider the *Psychological Detective* activity on p. 344 in the textbook.

    B. Research Methods

        1. Longitudinal, Cross-Sectional, and Sequential Studies

II. Development from Conception to Birth

    A. Heredity

        1. Polygenic Heredity

        2. Determination of Sex

        3. Sex-Linked Traits

    B. Prenatal Development

        1. Barriers to Prenatal Development

2. Teratogens

3. Drugs

4. Smoking

5. Alcohol

6. Checking the Health of the Fetus

7. Ultrasound

8. Amniocentesis

Consider the *Study Tip* on p. 352 in the textbook.

III. Development in Infancy

    A. Sensory Abilities

        1. Hearing and Voice Recognition

        2. Vision

        3. Taste and Smell

B. How Newborns Learn

    1. Classical Conditioning

Consider the *Psychological Detective* activity on p. 353 in the textbook.

    2. Operant Conditioning

    3. Imitating Others

C. Maturation

    1. Development of the Brain

    2. Physical Development

IV. Psychosocial Development in Childhood

A. Temperament

B. Personality Development

    1. Sigmund Freud

    2. Erik Erikson

C. Attachment

      1. Ethological Theory

      2. The Strange Situation Test

D. The Father's Role

E. Day Care

F. The Peer Group

G. Television

Consider the *Psychological Detective* activity on p. 363 in the textbook.

V. Cognitive Development in Childhood

    A. Piaget's Theory

      1. The Sensorimotor Stage

      2. The Preoperational Stage

3. The Concrete Operational Stage

4. Challenges to Piaget's Theory

Consider the *Study Tip* on p. 367 in the textbook.

B. Moral Development

VI. ADOLESCENCE

A. Physical Changes

B. Cognitive and Intellectual Changes

1. Adolescent Thought Patterns

C. Personality and Social Changes

1. Possible Outcomes of Identity Formation

2. Adolescent Peer Groups

3. Family Influences

4. Making a Commitment

VII. EARLY Adulthood

A. Physical Changes

B. Cognitive and Intellectual Changes

Consider the *Psychological Detective* activity on p. 376 in the textbook.

1. Types of Intelligence

C. Personality and Social Changes

1. Intimacy versus Isolation

2. Marriage

3. Children

4. Parenting Styles

5. The Feminization of Poverty

6. Career Development

VIII. Middle Adulthood

    A. Physical Changes

    B. Cognitive and Intellectual Changes

    C. Personality and Social Changes.

        1. Midlife Crisis

        2. Other Stresses during Middle Adulthood

Consider the *Psychological Detective* activity on p. 381 in the textbook.

IX. Late Adulthood

    A. Physical Changes

Consider the *Psychological Detective* activity on p. 384 in the textbook.

Complete the *Hands On* activity on p. 385 in the textbook.

       1. Alzheimer's Disease

       2. Culture and Life Expectancy

   B. Cognitive and Intellectual Changes

       1. Memory

       2. Ageism

Consider the *Study Tip* on p. 387 in the textbook.

   C. Personality and Social Changes

       1. Retirement

Consider the *Study Tip* on p. 389 in the textbook.

X. Death Dying, and Bereavement

    A. Attitudes toward Death

        1. Childhood

        2. Adolescence

        3. Young Adulthood

        4. Middle Adulthood

        5. Late Adulthood

    B. Confronting Death

        1. Confronting One's Own Death

    C. Bereavement, Grief, and Support

        1. Normal Grief and Complicated Grief

        2. Variables that Affect Grief

            a. Nature of the death

b. Nature of the deceased

c. Bereavement context

d. Nature of the bereaved

3. Hospice

4. Mourning

Chapter Test

In addition to completing the practice items that follow, remember to complete the items in the *Check Your Progress* sections in each chapter in the textbook. The answers to the **Multiple Choice Items**, **Completion Items**, and **Critical Thinking Exercises** are presented at the end of the **Chapter Test**.

Multiple Choice Items

Circle the letter that corresponds to the *best* alternative for each of the following items.

1. When considering developmental processes, nature refers to the
   a. theory that environmental factors determine physical and cognitive development.
   b. pattern of change in human capabilities that occurs at birth.
   c. process by which individuals adjust schemas to new information.
   d. theory that physical and cognitive development is genetically determined.

2. The research technique used when a developmental psychologist first surveys a sample of middle school students during the first week of school to learn how many have experimented with alcohol is a
   a. longitudinal study.
   b. cross-sectional study.
   c. sequential study.
   d. cohort study.

3. The research technique used when a developmental psychologist first surveys a sample of middle school students to learn how many have experimented with alcohol and then follows them for three years to learn how many experiment during that period is a
   a. longitudinal study.
   b. cross-sectional study.
   c. sequential study.
   d. cohort study.

4. Polygenic inheritance accounts for the inherited component of
   a. height.
   b. weight.
   c. facial features.
   d. intelligence.

5. A teratogen is
    a. any biological, chemical, or physical agent capable of causing a birth defect.
    b. a concept or framework that organizes or interprets information.
    c. the expression of an individual's genotype in measurable characteristics.
    d. the tendency for an infant to form an attachment to the first moving object it encounters.

6. Characteristics of a child who has fetal alcohol syndrome include
    a. normal heart function.
    b. low intelligence.
    c. large head circumference.
    d. normal hearing

7. The outline picture produced by projecting sound waves onto the fetus, uterus, and placenta is
    a. a sonogram.
    b. a genetic map.
    c. an amniocentesis scan.
    d. a myogram.

8. The reflex in which an infant's toes fan outward is the
    a. rooting reflex.
    b. palmar reflex.
    c. Moro reflex.
    d. Babinski reflex.

9. A 3-year-old child who is able to run faster and knows more words than other 3-year-olds is
    a. industrious.
    b. conventional.
    c. precocious.
    d. accommodating.

10. Infants who learn that needs like comfort, food, and warmth will be met by responsive caregivers have resolved Erikson's crisis of
    a. basic trust versus basic mistrust.
    b. autonomy versus shame and doubt.
    c. initiative versus guilt.
    d. industry versus inferiority.

11. Children who develop a sense of whether they control their behavior or whether others control it have resolved Erikson's crisis of
    a. basic trust versus basic mistrust.
    b. autonomy versus shame and doubt.
    c. initiative versus guilt.
    d. industry versus inferiority.

12. Children who believe they can act independently and have personal control over their actions have a feeling of
    a. industriousness.
    b. conventionality.
    c. precocity.
    d. autonomy.

13. Children begin to evaluate the consequences of their own behavior during Erikson's crisis of
    a. basic trust versus basic mistrust.
    b. autonomy versus shame and doubt.
    c. initiative versus guilt.
    d. industry versus inferiority.

14. Children begin to acquire the knowledge and skills to become productive members of society during Erikson's crisis of
    a. basic trust versus basic mistrust.
    b. autonomy versus shame and doubt.
    c. initiative versus guilt.
    d. industry versus inferiority.

15. The intense reciprocal relationship formed between a mother and her child is
    a. attachment.
    b. contact comfort.
    c. basic trust.
    d. autonomy.

16. Harlow's research with infant monkeys demonstrated the importance of
    a. critical periods.
    b. parenting style.
    c. contact comfort.
    d. peer groups.

17. A child who realizes that toys continue to exist even when they cannot be seen has developed the concept of
    a. accommodation.
    b. conservation.
    c. egocentrism.
    d. object permanence.

18. A child in Piaget's preoperational stage is
    a. logically manipulating mental representations.
    b. using symbolic representations to consider hypothetical situations.
    c. thinking about people and objects that are not present.
    d. exploring the environment using sensory and motor behavior.

19. After making two right turns on a walk around the block, a child who says that her house is still behind her is demonstrating
    a. accommodation.
    b. conservation.
    c. egocentrism.
    d. object permanence.

20. A child in Piaget's concrete operational stage is
    a. logically manipulating mental representations.
    b. using symbolic representations to consider hypothetical situations.
    c. thinking about people and objects that are not present.
    d. exploring the environment using sensory and motor behavior.

21. A second grader who realizes that rolling a ball of clay into a cylinder does not change the amount of clay has acquired the concept of
    a. centration.
    b. conservation.
    c. object permanence.
    d. assimilation.

22. A kindergartner who is in Kohlberg's preconventional stage of moral development would be expected to say
    a. "you just have to obey school rules"
    b. "if you don't tell on me, I won't tell on you"
    c. "I follow school rules because they are in everyone's best interest"
    d. "because my teachers will like me"

23. Parents noticing that their child is having a growth spurt have evidence that the child is entering
    a. adolescence.
    b. puberty.
    c. precocity.
    d. pubescence.

24. The term secular trend refers to the tendency
    a. for one generation to begin puberty earlier than their parents.
    b. of parents to adopt a laissez-faire parenting style.
    c. for children to behave according to the rules of conventional morality earlier.
    d. of pubescent children to conform to peer group values at an earlier age.

25. Primary sex characteristics include
    a. axillary and pubic hair.
    b. coarse, oily skin.
    c. mature testes and ovaries.
    d. disproportional feet.

26. A child in Piaget's formal operational stage is
    a. logically manipulating mental representations.
    b. using symbolic representations to consider hypothetical situations.
    c. thinking about people and objects that are not present.
    d. exploring the environment using sensory and motor behavior.

27. The feeling of invincibility experienced by many adolescents may be attributable to
    a. the personal fable.
    b. an imaginary audience.
    c. fluid intelligence.
    d. the secular trend.

28. The excessive concern about personal appearance experienced by many adolescents may be attributable to
    a. the personal fable.
    b. an imaginary audience.
    c. fluid intelligence.
    d. the secular trend.

29. Adolescents wondering who they are and what they will ultimately do in life are confronting Erikson's crisis of
    a. identity versus identity confusion.
    b. intimacy versus isolation.
    c. generativity versus stagnation.
    d. integrity versus despair.

30. Foreclosure in adolescence refers to
    a. adoption of behaviors opposite of those expected.
    b. failure to develop an identity due to apathy.
    c. trying several identities with no intention to select one.
    d. uncritical adoption of parental values and desires.

31. The type of intelligence required when students are required to solve spatial relations problems they have never encountered before is
    a. verbal intelligence
    b. unbiased intelligence
    c. fluid intelligence
    d. crystallized intelligence

32. The type of intelligence required when students are required apply knowledge they have learned through life experiences like the temperature at which water boils is
    a. verbal intelligence
    b. unbiased intelligence
    c. fluid intelligence
    d. crystallized intelligence

33. Young adults wondering who, or if, they will marry are confronting Erikson's crisis of
    a. identity versus identity confusion.
    b. intimacy versus isolation.
    c. generativity versus stagnation.
    d. integrity versus despair.

34. Adults wondering how their children will fare in life are confronting Erikson's crisis of
    a. identity versus identity confusion.
    b. intimacy versus isolation.
    c. generativity versus stagnation.
    d. integrity versus despair.

35. A person in middle adulthood can reasonably expect to deal with
    a. the empty nest syndrome.
    b. issues of intimacy or isolation.
    c. dementia.
    d. ageism.

36. The general intellectual decline associated with old age is
    a. ageism.
    b. foreclosure.
    c. dementia.
    d. identity diffusion.

37. A business that has a mandatory retirement age may be guilty of
    a. ageism.
    b. foreclosure.
    c. negative identity.
    d. identity diffusion.

38. Older adults reflecting on the value of their lives are confronting Erikson's crisis of
    a. identity versus identity confusion.
    b. intimacy versus isolation.
    c. generativity versus stagnation.
    d. integrity versus despair.

39. The emotional and psychological reactions to losing someone through death are
    a. bereavement.
    b. grief.
    c. mourning.
    d. complicated grief.

40. The behavioral changes after losing someone through death are
    a. bereavement.
    b. grief.
    c. mourning.
    d. complicated grief.

Completion Items

Complete the following statements with key terms or concepts from the textbook.

1. The theory that physical and cognitive development is determined by environmental factors is _____.

2. The field that studies the influences of heredity and environment on behavior is _____.

3. A psychologist who identifies a group of kindergartners and collects data from them at least once a year until they leave high school is conducting a(n) _____ study.

4. A specific time during development when damage may occur of certain processes should take place is a(n) _____.

5. Withdrawal of amniotic fluid to detect genetic abnormalities in the fetus is _____.

6. An infant turns its head on the direction of a touch on the face due to the _____ reflex.

7. An infant's strong grip on a parent's finger is due to the grasping or _____ reflex.

8. An infant who is startled by a loud noise is demonstrating the _____ reflex.

9. The biological unfolding of the genetic plan for an individual's development is _____.

10. Piaget's term for the process of incorporating information into existing schemas is _____.

11. Piaget's term for the capacity to alter existing schemas to understand new information is _____.

12. A young child who can think about an object that is not present can make a(n) _____.

13. A child who can use a mental thought or activity as a substitute for an actual object can make a(n) _____.

14. A middle school student who says, "You just have to obey school rules" is in Kohlberg's stage of_____.

15. The time at which a person achieves sexual maturity is _____.

16. The beginning of menstruation is the _____.

17. Coarse, oily skin and auxiliary and pubic hair are _____.

18. An adolescent who adopts a set of well-chosen values and goals is said to have reached _____.

19. An adolescent who adopts behaviors that are opposite of what is expected has a(n) _____.

20. An adolescent's failure to develop an identity due to a lack of goals and general apathy is _____.

21. A period in which an adolescent tries several identities without intending to settle on a particular one is a(n) _____.

22. Farsightedness that develops during middle adulthood is _____.

23. The hearing disorder experienced by many middle-aged adults is _____.

24. The cessation of ovulation and menstruation is _____.

25. A "50 something" woman who falls and breaks her pelvis may have _____.

26. A "40 something" man who begins to consider mortality and decides to change jobs, even if the change requires relocation, is having a(n) _____.

27. An elderly person experiencing clouding of the lens of one or both eyes has _____.

28. The degenerative brain disorder that results I progressive loss of intelligence and awareness is_____.

29. Losing someone through death is _____.

30. An institution where terminally ill patients and their families receive warm, friendly, personalized care is a(n) _____.

Critical Thinking Exercises

A couple expecting a baby within the next few months is trying to decide whether to use day care or to take time off from their careers to care for their child. In speaking to friends and relatives about this issue, they realize that the topic of day care is very controversial and many of their friends hold strong views on both sides of the debate. What information presented in this chapter might help the couple make their decision?

An elderly person is concerned about the effects of aging on his memory. What information presented in this chapter about Alzheimer's disease would help this person understand the effects of aging on memory?

Chapter Test Answers
Multiple Choice Items

1. d	11. b	21. b	31. c
2. b	12. d	22. b	32. d
3. c	13. c	23. d	33. b
4. d	14. d	24. a	34. c
5. a	15. a	25. c	35. a
6. b	16. c	26. b	36. c
7. a	17. d	27. a	37. a
8. d	18. c	28. b	38. d
9. c	19. c	29. a	39. b
10. a	20. a	30. d	40. c

Completion Items

1. nurture	11. accommodation	21. moratorium
2. behavior genetics	12. mental representation	22. presbyopia
3. longitudinal	13. symbolic representation	23. presbycusis
4. critical period	14. conventional role conformity	24. menopause
5. amniocentesis	15. puberty	25. osteoporosis
6. rooting	16. menarche	26. midlife crisis
7. palmar	17. secondary sex characteristics	27. cataracts
8. Moro	18. identity achievement	28. Alzheimer's disease
9. maturation	19. negative identity	29. bereavement
10. assimilation	20. identity diffusion	30. hospice

Critical Thinking Exercises

1. Most researchers today agree that the quality of childcare arrangements is the key factor in promoting secure attachment in early childhood and preventing later problems. Many studies have found that children who experience high quality day care tend to be more sociable, better adjusted, and more academically competent than children who have experienced poor quality daycare. To date, no significant negative long-term negative effects have been found in children who have had high quality daycare experiences. Important factors in high-quality day care include: 1) warm, responsive caregivers, 2) developmentally appropriate activities, equipment and materials, 3) caregivers trained in early childhood development, and 4) low turnover and staff-to-child ratios of 1 to 5.

2. David Snowdon from the University of Kentucky studied 678 Sisters of Notre Dame, and found that some developed Alzheimer's disease while others did not. Some of the factors identified as significant in the nuns who lived into their nineties without any sign of the disease included staying mentally active, expressing positive emotions, and including folic acid in their diet.

Key Vocabulary Terms: The terms listed in the margins of pages and entered in **boldface** type in the textbook are listed below with space for you to write the definitions. Remember that you may also want to create a list of the terms entered in italics in the textbook, especially those your instructor mentions in lectures. Again, you should try to write definitions *in your own words* because translating the terms into familiar language will facilitate retention.

lifespan developmental psychology

nature

nurture

behavior genetics

longitudinal study

cross-sectional study

sequential studies

cohort

zygote

mitosis

embryo

chromosomes

genes

deoxyribonucleic acid (DNA)

polygenic inheritance

fetus

placenta

teratogen

critical period

fetal alcohol syndrome (FAS)

ultrasound procedure

sonogram

amniocentesis

rooting reflex

palmar or grasp reflex

Moro reflex

Babinski reflex

maturation

precocious

psychosocial crisis

basic trust versus basic mistrust

autonomy versus shame and doubt

autonomy

initiative versus guilt

industry versus inferiority

attachment

contact comfort

ethological theory of attachment

peer group

cognitive development

assimilation

accommodation

sensorimotor stage

object permanence

mental representation

preoperational stage

symbolic representation

egocentrism

concrete operational stage

conservation

preconventional level

conventional role conformity

postconventional level/autonomous moral principles

adolescence

pubescence

puberty

secular trend

primary sex characteristics

menarche

secondary sex characteristics

formal operational stage

personal fable

imaginary audience

identity versus identity confusion

identity achievement

foreclosure

negative identity

identity diffusion

moratorium

early adulthood

fluid intelligence

crystallized intelligence

emotional intelligence

intimacy versus isolation

middle adulthood

presbyopia

presbycusis

menopause

osteoporosis

midlife crisis

generativity versus stagnation

empty nest syndrome

late adulthood

cataracts

dementia

Alzheimer's disease

ageism

integrity versus despair

bereavement

bereaved

grief

mourning

complicated grief

hospice

CHAPTER 10

Sex and Gender

Notes from Class and the Textbook

Use the space provided in this outline to record notes from the textbook as well as from class lectures and discussion.

I. Sex and Gender: An Introduction

    A. The Biology of Sex

        1. The Genetics of Sex

        2. Genetic Abnormalities

        3. Male Vulnerability

Consider the *Study Tip* on p. 398 in the textbook.

    B. Sexual Orientation

    C. Sexual Behavior

        1. Differences in Sexual Attitudes and Practices

        2. Sexual Dysfunctions

    D. The Development of Gender Roles

1. Psychodynamic Theory

Consider the *Psychological Detective* activity on p. 406 in the textbook.

2. Observational Learning

3. Cognitive Developmental Theory

4. Gender Schema Theory

D. Gender Stereotyping

Consider the *Study Tip* on p. 407 in the textbook.

E. Cultural Differences in Views of Masculinity and Femininity

Consider the *Psychological Detective* activity on p. 408 in the textbook.

1. Mass Media and Gender Stereotypes

II. Similarities and Differences between Males and Females

    A. Biological Differences: Fact and Fiction

        1. Brain Differences

    B. Early Analyses of Sex Differences

    C. The Cognitive Realm

        1. Verbal Abilities

        2. Mathematical Abilities

        3. Visual-Spatial Abilities

Consider the *Psychological Detective* activity on p. 416 in the textbook.

    D. The Social Realm

        1. Communication

        2. Helping Behavior

        3. Aggression

Consider the *Study Tip* on p. 417 in the textbook.

III. Social Issues

    A. Education

        1. Elementary School

Consider the *Psychological Detective* activity on p. 420 in the textbook.

        2. High School and Higher Education

Consider the *Study Tip* on p. 421 in the textbook.

    B. Work and Careers

        1. Sexual Harassment

2. Frequency of Sexual Harassment

3. Perceiving Sexual Harassment

4. Gender Stereotyping on the Job

5. Women as Leaders

C. Family Responsibilities

1. Juggling

Chapter Test

In addition to completing the practice items that follow, remember to complete the items in the *Check Your Progress* sections in each chapter in the textbook. The answers to the **Multiple Choice Items**, **Completion Items**, and **Critical Thinking Exercises** are presented at the end of the **Chapter Test**.

Multiple Choice Items

Circle the letter that corresponds to the *best* alternative for each of the following items.

1. The term that would be relevant in a discussion of sex is
   a. color preference.
   b. relationship maintenance.
   c. genitalia.
   d. career choice.

2. A discussion of gender might include a statement like
   a. "girls wear pink."
   b. "men have higher levels of testosterone."
   c. "women have two X chromosomes."
   d. "the protein is H-Y antigen."

3. An individual who has both ovarian and testicular tissue
   a. has Turner syndrome.
   b. lacks the H-Y antigen.
   c. is a hermaphrodite.
   d. has androgen insensitivity syndrome.

4. A pseudohermaphrodite is characterized by
   a. external genitalia that do not match their chromosomal makeup.
   b. very high levels of H-Y antigen.
   c. a combination of male and female external genitalia.
   d. an XYY chromosome pattern.

5. Adrenogenital syndrome is a condition in which
   a. females develop adrenal glands in place of genitals.
   b. females develop genitals resembling those of males.
   c. people have the functional reproductive anatomy of both sexes.
   d. males develop secondary sex characteristics resembling those of females.

6. Androgen insensitivity syndrome occurs when
   a. female embryos respond to male hormones.
   b. female embryos do not respond to female hormones.
   c. male embryos respond to female hormones.
   d. male embryos do not respond to male hormones.

7. Initial erection of the penis occurs in the
   a. excitement stage.
   b. plateau stage.
   c. orgasm stage.
   d. resolution stage.

8. A woman experiences a sex-tension flash in the
   a. excitement stage.
   b. plateau stage.
   c. orgasm stage.
   d. resolution stage.

9. The increase in blood flow to the genitals during the excitement stage of the sexual response cycle is
   a. myotonia.
   b. vasocongestion.
   c. refraction.
   d. resolution.

10. The involuntary rhythmic muscle contractions during the orgasm stage of the sexual response cycle result from
    a. myotonia.
    b. vasocongestion.
    c. refraction.
    d. resolution.

11. The sexually transmitted infection known as the "great imitator" is
    a. bacterial vaginosis.
    b. genital herpes.
    c. gonorrhea.
    d. syphilis.

12. A man who experiences pain while urinating and notices a white, yellow, or green discharge from the penis has
    a. chlamydia.
    b. genital herpes.
    c. gonorrhea.
    d. syphilis.

13. The sexually transmitted infection characterized by blisters followed by sores that may last 2-4 weeks is
    a. chlamydia.
    b. genital herpes.
    c. gonorrhea.
    d. syphilis.

14. Hypoactive sexual disorder is characterized by
    a. genital pain associated with sexual intercourse.
    b. active avoidance of genital sexual contact with a sexual partner.
    c. inability to attain or maintain an adequate lubrication-swelling response.
    d. deficient or absent sexual fantasies or desire for sexual activity.

15. Sexual aversion disorder is characterized by
    a. genital pain associated with sexual intercourse.
    b. active avoidance of genital sexual contact with a sexual partner.
    c. inability to attain or maintain an adequate lubrication-swelling response.
    d. deficient or absent sexual fantasies or desire for sexual activity.

16. Dyspareunia is characterized by
    a. genital pain associated with sexual intercourse.
    b. active avoidance of genital sexual contact with a sexual partner.
    c. inability to attain or maintain an adequate lubrication-swelling response.
    d. deficient or absent sexual fantasies or desire for sexual activity.

17. The gender-schema theory for explaining the development of gender distinctions states that people
    a. learn expectations about masculine and feminine attributes that influence memory, perception, and behavior.
    b. develop cognitive factors that give rise to gender identity, gender stability, and gender constancy.
    c. exert control over secondary sex characteristics based on external events.
    d. primary sex characteristics develop in response to predictable environmental stimuli.

18. A man who insists that men are better drivers than women is expressing
    a. a gender stereotype.
    b. gender discrimination.
    c. hostile sexism.
    d. gender prejudice.

19. The most consistent finding concerning spatial ability is that
    a. males and females score alike.
    b. males outperform females on mental rotation tasks.
    c. females outperform males at identifying directions.
    d. females outperform males in solving jigsaw puzzles.

20. Research comparing males and females shows that
    a. males earn higher scores on standardized intelligence tests.
    b. females talk more than males.
    c. females earn higher grades in math in school.
    d. males show higher levels of relational aggression.

21. A psychologist investigating sexism in the classroom could expect to observe instructors
    a. making more eye contact with women.
    b. calling on women more than men.
    c. calling women by name more often.
    d. addressing classes as if only men are present.

22. A woman who is told that she will be demoted or fired if she does not have sexual intercourse with her supervisor is a victim of
   a. sexual assault.
   b. standard gender stereotyping.
   c. quid pro quo harassment.
   d. hostile work environment harassment.

23. The assistant principle for discipline in a school makes frequent remarks about a teacher's body and takes every opportunity to stand close to her. Although he has never touched her inappropriately, she feels very uncomfortable and is hesitant to ask for his assistance if she encounters a problem in her classroom. The man's behavior is an example of
   a. sexual assault.
   b. standard gender stereotyping.
   c. quid pro quo harassment.
   d. hostile work environment harassment.

24. Self-reported data on child-care involvement has indicated that
   a. men and women are more likely to share child care than household chores.
   b. men tend to have far greater levels of involvement in child care in every category.
   c. women tend to have far greater levels of involvement in child care in every category.
   d. women tend to do more of the child care related tasks that were rated as unpleasant.

25. Research on the impact of juggling multiple (job- and home-related) tasks suggests that
   a. men seem better equipped to take on a variety of tasks than women.
   b. women seem better equipped to take on a variety of tasks than men.
   c. juggling multiple roles seems to insulate women and men against depression.
   d. juggling multiple tasks is the single leading cause of depression in American women.

Completion Items

Complete the following statements with key terms or concepts from the textbook.

1. The distinction between men and women based on biological factors is _____.

2. Social and psychological phenomena associated with being feminine or masculine define _____.

3. Persons born with mixtures of male and female biological characteristics are _____.

4. People with one testis and one ovary are _____.

5. People whose external genitalia and secondary sex characteristics do not match their chromosomal makeup are _____.

6. If the HY antigen is present during the seventh week of embryonic development, the child will be _____.

7. An individual's erotic and emotional feelings for same-sex or opposite-sex individuals are _____.

8. The condition caused by exposure to excessive amounts of androgens during the fetal period can result in females with genitalia resembling those of males is _____.

9. Failure of a male embryo to respond to male hormones is _____.

10. The last stage of the sexual response cycle is the _____ stage.

11. A woman who is unaware that she has a sexually transmitted infection most likely has _____.

12. Boys are less likely to enroll in home economics courses and girls are less likely to work in construction because of _____.

13. A set of beliefs about members of a particular group is a(n) _____.

14. Differential treatment of an individual on the basis of his or her sex is _____.

15. A supervisor who tells "dirty" joke to employees of the opposite sex is committing _____ sexual harassment.

Critical Thinking Exercise

The term *critical thinking* is so commonplace that it has become a cliché. It is frequently used because it describes so well a process that is important in innumerable ways. Consider definitions of the two words that comprise the term. Critical means *requiring careful judgment.* Thinking means *to form or have in the mind.* Thus, *critical thinking* means *having careful judgment in the mind.*

Critical thinking is represented in good communication of all forms: reading, listening, speaking, and writing. Part of the active reading process is to consider carefully that which you read. Likewise, a good listener does not merely soak up information like a sponge, but listens while attending to all the subtleties of meaning in the message. When one person communicates with others, verbally or in writing, it is important that the message reflect both logical reasoning and appropriate expression of the person's conclusions. Be cautious about making or conveying assumptions.

For example, a report in a newspaper stated that boys who play with dolls when they are young are more likely to grow up to be homosexual. Here are some questions readers should ask while reading the article:
What is the average population rate for homosexuality in males?
Was this population rate different from the study's rate of homosexuality?
How were the boys selected to participate in the study?
Were the boys given surveys to complete, or were they observed playing with dolls?
Were the boys studied over a long period of time, i.e. enrolled in a longitudinal study, or were they surveyed only once in adulthood?
How were "dolls" defined in this study?

Based on the correlational study, the conclusion that playing with dolls as a young boy causes adult men to become homosexual cannot be supported.

Chapter Test Answers

Multiple Choice Items

1. c	6. d	11. d	16. a	21. d
2. a	7. a	12. c	17. a	22. c
3. c	8. b	13. b	18. a	23. d
4. a	9. b	14. d	19. b	24. d
5. b	10. a	15. b	20. c	25. c

Completion Items

1. sex	6. male	11. Chlamydia
2. gender	7. sexual orientation	12. gender roles
3. intersexes	8. androgenital syndrome	13. stereotype
4. hermaphrodites	9. androgen insensitivity syndrome	14. sexism
5. pseudohermaphrodites	10. resolution	15. hostile environment

Critical Thinking Exercise
Response contained in exercise above.

Key Vocabulary Terms: The terms listed in the margins of pages and entered in **boldface** type in the textbook are listed below with space for you to write the definitions. Remember that you may also want to create a list of the terms entered in italics in the textbook, especially those your instructor mentions in lectures. Again, you should try to write definitions *in your own words* because translating the terms into familiar language will facilitate retention.

sex

gender

hermaphrodite

pseudohermaphrodite

sexual orientation

adrenogenital syndrome

androgen insensitivity syndrome

gender roles

cognitive developmental theory

gender-schema theory

stereotype

sexism

sexual harassment

CHAPTER 11

Personality

Notes from Class and the Textbook
Use the space provided in this outline to record notes from the textbook as well as from class lectures and discussion.

I. Analyzing Personality

    A. Defining Personality

    B. Assessing Personality

        1. Self-Report Inventories

        2. The Minnesota Multiphasic Personality Inventory

        3. The California Psychological Inventory

        4. Limitations of Self-Report Inventories

        5. Projective Tests

        6. Limitations of Projective Tests

        7. The Barnum Effect

Consider the *Psychological Detective* activity on p. 437 in the textbook.

        8. Other Measures

C. Is Behavior Consistent?

1. Challenges to the Idea of Consistency

2. In Defense of Consistency

Consider the *Psychological Detective* activity on p. 438 in the textbook.

3. Evidence of Consistency Based on Multiple Measures

D. Evaluating Personality Theories

Consider the *Study Tip* on p. 440 in the textbook.

II. Trait Approaches

Complete the *Hands On* activity on p. 440 in the textbook.

A. Factors in Personality: Raymond B. Cattell

B. Categorization of Traits: Hans Eysenck

C. The "Big Five" Traits

Consider the *Study Tip* on p. 444 in the textbook.

D. Alternatives to the Big Five

III. Biological Factors in Personality

A. Early Biological Approaches

Complete the *Myth or Science* activity on p. 447 in the textbook.

1. Humors and Bumps

2. Body Types

3. Sensation Seeking

Complete the *Hands On* activity on p. 449 in the textbook.

B. Twin Studies

Consider the *Study Tip* on p. 450 in the textbook.

Complete the *Psychological Detective* activity on p. 451 in the textbook.

        C. Personality and the Evolutionary Perspective

IV. The Psychodynamic Perspective

    A. Basic Concepts

        1. Psychic Determinism

Complete the *Psychological Detective* activity on p. 455 in the textbook.

        2. Instincts

        3. The Unconscious

    B. The Structure of the Mind

        1. The Id

2. The Ego

3. The Superego

4. Interaction of Id, Ego, and Superego

C. Defense Mechanisms

Complete the *Psychological Detective* activity on p. 457 in the textbook.

D. Stages of Psychosexual Development

1. The Oral Stage

2. The Anal Stage

3. The Phallic Stage

4. The Latency and Genital Stages

E. Freud in Perspective

Consider the *Study Tip* on p. 460 in the textbook.

F. The Neo-Freudians

    1. Evaluation of Freudian Theory

V. The Behavioral Perspective

    A. Basic Premises

    B. Application and Evaluation

VI. The Social – Cognitive Perspective

    A. Learning and Cognitive Perspectives

        1. Rotter's Social Learning Theory

        2. Bandura's Social Cognitive Theory

Consider the *Study Tip* on p. 467 in the textbook.

VII. The Humanistic Perspective

    A. Abraham Maslow

        1. Basic Needs

        2. Self-Actualization

    B. Carl Rogers

Chapter Test

In addition to completing the practice items that follow, remember to complete the items in the *Check Your Progress* sections in each chapter in the textbook. The answers to the **Multiple Choice Items**, **Completion Items**, and **Critical Thinking Exercises** are presented at the end of the **Chapter Test**.

Multiple Choice Items

Circle the letter that corresponds to the *best* alternative for each of the following items.

1. Students experiencing test anxiety who respond to an instrument comprised of statements about personal behaviors are completing
    a. a projective test.
    b. an achievement test.
    c. a self-report-inventory.
    d. an opinion survey.

2. People experiencing serious depression who respond to an instrument comprised of ambiguous stimuli are completing
    a. a projective test.
    b. an achievement test.
    c. a self-report-inventory.
    d. an opinion survey.

3. The tendency to accept generalized personality descriptions as accurate descriptions of oneself is
    a. The Freud problem.
    b. fixation.
    c. psychic determinism.
    d. the Barnum effect.

4. The parsimony of a personality theory refers to its
    a. simplicity.
    b. influence on future research.
    c. research support.
    d. practical applications.

5. The heuristic function of a personality theory refers to its
    a. simplicity.
    b. influence on future research.
    c. research support.
    d. practical applications.

6. When one student describes another student as introverted, introversion is
    a. a conscious motivation.
    b. a fixation.
    c. a situational influence.
    d. a trait.

7. The "Big Five" trait that would be applied to a person who is organized, dependable, competent, and responsible is
    a. extraversion.
    b. agreeableness.
    c. conscientiousness.
    d. openness to experience.

8. The "Big Five" trait that would be applied to a person who is self-defeating, anxious, and concerned about personal adequacy is
   a. neuroticism.
   b. agreeableness.
   c. conscientiousness.
   d. openness to experience.

9. The "Big Five" trait that would be applied to a person who has an appreciation for knowledge and has nontraditional values is
   a. neuroticism.
   b. agreeableness.
   c. conscientiousness.
   d. openness to experience.

10. A dimension of personality produced by clinical judgment and sorting that would explain an adult who has fragmented thoughts and perceptions due to past sexual abuse is
   a. dysphoria.
   b. emotional dysregulation.
   c. dissociated consciousness.
   d. thought disorder.

11. A dimension of personality produced by clinical judgment and sorting that would explain a person who has temper tantrums is
   a. dysphoria.
   b. emotional dysregulation.
   c. dissociated consciousness.
   d. thought disorder.

12. A dimension of personality produced by clinical judgment and sorting that would explain a person who is self-important and that the function of other people to serve as an audience is
   a. dysphoria.
   b. obsessionality
   c. narcissism.
   d. thought disorder.

13. The perspective on personality based on describing the major dimensions on which individuals differ is the
   a. biological perspective.
   b. behavioral perspective.
   c. social-cognitive perspective.
   d. trait perspective.

14. Sensation seeking through social activities such as parties is
   a. thrill seeking.
   b. boredom susceptibility.
   c. disinhibition.
   d. experience seeking.

15. Sensation seeking through activities like bridge jumping or skydiving is
   a. thrill seeking.
   b. boredom susceptibility.
   c. disinhibition.
   d. experience seeking.

16. The assumption that all behavior is a result of early childhood experiences is
    a. reciprocal determinism.
    b. rationalization.
    c. psychic determinism.
    d. self-actualization.

17. In psychodynamic theory, the id operates according to the
    a. pleasure principle.
    b. reality principle.
    c. moral principle.
    d. idealism principle.

18. In psychodynamic theory, the ego operates according to the
    a. pleasure principle.
    b. reality principle.
    c. moral principle.
    d. idealism principle.

19. In psychodynamic theory, the superego includes the
    a. unconscious.
    b. executive of the personality.
    c. instincts.
    d. ego ideal.

20. After doing badly on a psychology test, a student who yells at her roommate and hangs up in the middle of a phone conversation with her parents is exhibiting
    a. denial.
    b. displacement.
    c. rationalization.
    d. regression.

21. Another student who did badly on the same psychology test who tells his roommate that he doesn't care because he didn't want to be a psychologist anyway is exhibiting
    a. denial.
    b. displacement.
    c. rationalization.
    d. regression.

22. A third student who did badly on the same psychology test who returns to his room yelling and screaming, throws his book, and punches the wall is exhibiting
    a. denial.
    b. displacement.
    c. rationalization.
    d. regression.

23. A person is excessively dependent and overeats is fixated at the
    a. oral stage of psychosexual development.
    b. anal stage of psychosexual development.
    c. phallic stage of psychosexual development.
    d. genital stage of psychosexual development.

24. A person whose parents were very strict during toilet training and becomes overly neat and orderly is fixated at the
    a. oral stage of psychosexual development.
    b. anal stage of psychosexual development.
    c. phallic stage of psychosexual development.
    d. genital stage of psychosexual development.

25. The perspective on personality adds ideas about how people thing to principles of learning is the
    a. biological perspective.
    b. behavioral perspective.
    c. social-cognitive perspective.
    d. trait perspective.

26. An employee who believes she received a raise because of her performance has
    a. a strong ego ideal.
    b. an overbearing conscience.
    c. an internal locus of control.
    d. a weak sense of self-efficacy.

27. The belief that all personal and situational variables and behavior interact constantly is
    a. reciprocal determinism.
    b. rationalization.
    c. psychic determinism.
    d. self-actualization.

28. People who believe that they can cope with most situations they encounter in life have
    a. a strong ego ideal.
    b. an overbearing conscience.
    c. an external locus of control.
    d. a strong sense of self-efficacy.

29. Humanistic psychologists believe that
    a. behavior is controlled by the unconscious.
    b. reinforcement and punishment determine behavior.
    c. people control their own behavior.
    d. learning occurs through watching and imitating others.

30. The need to develop one's full potential is
    a. reciprocal determinism.
    b. rationalization.
    c. psychic determinism.
    d. self-actualization.

Completion Items

Complete the following statements with key terms or concepts from the textbook.

1. A psychological test in which people are asked to answer true-false questions about themselves is a(n) _____.

2. The Rorschach Inkblot Test is an example of a(n) _____.

3. Carnival fortunetellers appear able to predict people's behavior because they rely on the _____.

4. The degree to which a personality theory is supported by scientific research results is its _____.

5. Describing a person as extraverted is describing the person on the basis of a(n) _____.

6. According to the "Big Five" trait theory, people who are fundamentally altruistic and considerate will have high scores on _____.

7. A psychologist describing a person as lacking remorse and impulsive is describing a person with _____.

8. A person who is absorbed by details, stingy, and has an excessive concern for cleanliness is demonstrating _____.

9. The study of personality based on analyzing bumps and indentations on the skull was _____.

10. The part of a person's personality that is outside awareness is the _____.

11. If a student channels aggressive impulses into the socially acceptable outlet of club rugby, the student is using the defense mechanism of _____.

12. People whose development is arrested at a stage of psychosexual development and who continue to display those behaviors as adults have developed a(n) _____.

13. The process in which a boy who wishes to possess his mother sexually and then identifies with his father for fear of retaliation is the _____.

14. The process in which a girl wishes to possess her father sexually is the _____.

15. The stage of psychosexual development characterized by a low level of sexual interest is the _____.

16. The stage of psychosexual development characterized by development of mature sexual interest is the _____.

17. Jung's conception of a component of the personality that contains images shared by all people is the _____.

18. The perspective on personality theory associated with behavior modification is the _____ perspective.

19. The concept based on whether people see their behavior as controlled by internal or external factors is _____.

20. Roger's concept that people should be accepted for what they are, not what others would like them to be is _____.

Critical Thinking Exercise

Read the following statements and determine which personality theorist would be most likely to make each statement.

Statement: Assessing a potential Peace Corp Volunteer	Theorist
"I would predict that if we can assess the candidate's levels of extroversion, neuroticism, aggression and empathy, we can probably predict how he/she will function overall"	
"His/her ability to function as a volunteer will depend on the interaction of behavior, cognitive ability, and environmental factors – a sort of reciprocal determinism"	
"Since all people have an innate drive to maximize their potential, I predict that this candidate will follow his/her drive to self actualize and become the best volunteer they can be"	
"If we can provide for this volunteer's basic needs: food and water, shelter, and safety. They will then have the energy to pursue self-actualization and become an excellent volunteer"	
"It really depends on how the candidate negotiated and resolved conflicts early in life and whether he/she has any unresolved unconscious conflicts"	

Chapter Test Answers

Multiple Choice Items

1. c	11. b	21. c
2. a	12. c	22. d
3. d	13. d	23. a
4. a	14. c	24. b
5. b	15. a	25. c
6. d	16. c	26. c
7. c	17. a	27. a
8. a	18. b	28. d
9. d	19. d	29. c
10. c	20. b	30. d

Completion Items

1. self-report inventory	11. sublimation
2. projective test	12. fixation
3. Barnum effect	13. Oedipal complex
4. empirical validity	14. Electra complex
5. trait	15. latency stage
6. agreeableness	16. genital stage
7. psychopathy	17. collective unconscious
8. obsessionality	18. behavioral
9. phrenology	19. locus of control
10. unconscious	20. unconditional positive regard

Critical Thinking Exercise

Statement: Assessing a potential Peace Corp Volunteer	Theorist
"I would predict that if we can assess the candidate's levels of extroversion, neuroticism, aggression and empathy, we can probably predict how he/she will function overall"	Hans Eysenck Trait
"His/her ability to function as a volunteer will depend on the interaction of behavior, cognitive ability, and environmental factors – a sort of reciprocal determinism"	Albert Bandura Social-Cognitive
"Since all people have an innate drive to maximize their potential, I predict that this candidate will follow his/her drive to self actualize and become the best volunteer they can be"	Carl Rogers Humanist
"If we can provide for this volunteer's basic needs: food and water, shelter, and safety. They will then have the energy to pursue self-actualization and become an excellent volunteer"	Abraham Maslow Hunmanist
"It really depends on how the candidate negotiated and resolved conflicts early in life and whether he/she has any unresolved unconscious conflicts"	Sigmund Freud

Key Vocabulary Terms: The terms listed in the margins of pages and entered in **boldface** type in the textbook are listed below with space for you to write the definitions. Remember that you may also want to create a list of the terms entered in italics in the textbook, especially those your instructor mentions in lectures. Again, you should try to write definitions *in your own words* because translating the terms into familiar language will facilitate retention.

personality

self-report inventory

projective test

Barnum effect

trait

psychic determinism

unconscious

id

ego

superego

defense mechanism

oral stage

fixation

anal stage

phallic stage

Oedipal complex

Electra complex

latency stage

genital stage

social learning theory

locus of control

reciprocal determinism

self-efficacy

humanistic psychology

self-actualization

CHAPTER 12

Psychological Disorders

Notes from Class and the Textbook
Use the space provided in this outline to record notes from the textbook as well as from class lectures and discussion.

I. Abnormal Behavior

    A. Criteria of Abnormality

        1. Statistical Rarity

        2. Interference with Normal Functioning

        3. Distress

        4. Deviance from Social Norms

    B. A Working Definition

    C. The Concept of Insanity

Consider the *Psychological Detective* activity on p. 475 in the textbook.

    D. Models of Abnormal Behavior

        1. The Medical Model

        2. The Psychological Models

3. Culture and Disorders

II. Classifying and Counting Psychological Disorders

Consider the *Study Tip* on p. 477 in the textbook.

A. *DSM-IV-TR*

B. The Labeling Issue

C. The Prevalence of Psychological Disorders

What tools, methods, and techniques are available to diagnose and determine the prevalence of psychological disorders?

III. Anxiety, Somatoform, and Dissociative Disorders

A. Anxiety Disorders

1. Phobias

2. Panic Disorder

Consider the *Psychological Detective* activity on p. 486 in the textbook.

3. Generalized Anxiety Disorder (GAD)

4. Obsessive—Compulsive Disorder

Consider the *Psychological Detective* activity on p. 488 in the textbook.

5. Posttraumatic Stress Disorder (PTSD)

B. Somatoform Disorders

1. Hypochondriasis

2. Somatization Disorder

3. Conversion Disorder

C. Dissociative Disorders

1. Dissociative Amnesia and Dissociative Fugue

Consider the *Psychological Detective* activity on p. 492 in the textbook.

2. Dissociative Identity Disorder

3. Depersonalization Disorders

Consider the *Study Tip* on p. 494 in the textbook.

IV. Mood Disorders

    A. Major Depressive Disorder

        1. Symptoms

        2. Prevalence and Course

        3. Suicide

Complete the *Myth or Science* activity on pp. 501-502 in the textbook.

    B. Bipolar Disorder

    C. Causes of Mood Disorders

        1. Biological Explanations

        2. The Psychodynamic Explanation

3. Cognitive and Behavioral Explanations

4. Multiple Causes

V. Schizophrenia

    A. Symptoms of Schizophrenia

        1. Positive Symptoms

        2. Negative Symptoms

    B. Subtypes of Schizophrenia

Consider the *Study Tip* on p. 513 in the textbook.

    C. Prevalence/Onset/Prognosis

    D. Causes of Schizophrenia

        1. Genetic Factors

Consider the *Psychological Detective* activity on p. 514 in the textbook.

        2. Brain Abnormalities

3. Neurotransmitters

4. Environmental Causes

5. Multiple Causes

VI. Personality Disorders, Sexual Disorders, and Substance Use Disorders

   A. Personality Disorders

Consider the *Psychological Detective* activity on p. 521 in the textbook.

   B. Sexual Disorders

      1. Gender Identity Disorder

      2. Paraphilias

      3. Fetishism

   C. Substance Use Disorders

Consider the *Study Tip* on p. 524 in the textbook.

Chapter Test

In addition to completing the practice items that follow, remember to complete the items in the *Check Your Progress* sections in each chapter of the textbook. The answers to the **Multiple Choice Items**, **Completion Items**, and **Critical Thinking Exercises** are presented at the end of the **Chapter Test**.

Multiple Choice Items

Circle the letter that corresponds to the *best* alternative for each of the following items.

1. The term insanity is
    a. a psychological diagnosis.
    b. a legal term.
    c. essentially a meaningless term.
    d. used only in clinical psychology.

2. The view that psychological disorders result from unconscious conflicts related to sex or aggression defines the
    a. medical model.
    b. psychodynamic model.
    c. cognitive model.
    d. sociocultural model.

3. The view that psychological disorders are learned and follow the principles of classical and operant conditioning defines the
    a. medical model.
    b. psychodynamic model.
    c. cognitive model.
    d. behavioral model.

4. A psychologist who has determined that a client has symptoms that meet the criteria of an existing classification system has
    a. made a diagnosis.
    b. defined prevalence.
    c. defined abnormal.
    d. calculated incidence.

5. A man who quits his job because he is afraid of riding in elevators has a
    a. panic disorder.
    b. conversion disorder.
    c. phobia.
    d. depersonalization disorder.

6. A woman who avoids going to movies or concerts because of her fear of being seen by others has
    a. arachnophobia.
    b. a social phobia.
    c. acrophobia.
    d. a specific phobia.

7. A man who turns down a promotion at work because he would have to work on the 50th floor of his company's office building has
    a. arachnophobia.
    b. a social phobia.
    c. acrophobia.
    d. a specific phobia.

8. The most serious anxiety disorder is
   a. panic disorder.
   b. generalized anxiety disorder.
   c. post traumatic stress disorder.
   d. somatization disorder.

9. A chronically high level of anxiety that is not attached to a specific stimulus is
   a. panic disorder.
   b. generalized anxiety disorder.
   c. post traumatic stress disorder.
   d. somatization disorder.

10. After stealing a textbook, a college student washes his hands every time he thinks about his behavior. The student's behavior is an example of
    a. a conversion disorder.
    b. a phobia.
    c. an anxiety disorder.
    d. an obsessive-compulsive disorder.

11. Somatoform disorders involve
    a. physical symptoms with no known medical cause.
    b. the irrational repetitive creation of somas.
    c. medical symptoms that are known to result from psychological issues.
    d. peculiar behaviors that are targeted at reducing anxiety about repetitive thoughts.

12. A person who makes frequent doctor visits because he is convinced that he has a serious cardiovascular disease probably has
    a. obsessive-compulsive disorder.
    b. cancer or a similarly serious disease.
    c. hypochrondriasis.
    d. a specific phobia.

13. A person who makes frequent doctor visits and consults pharmacists several times a week about what she can do to address a constellation of physical symptoms that most people would ignore probably has
    a. obsessive-compulsive disorder.
    b. cancer or a similarly serious disease.
    c. a somatization disorder.
    d. a specific phobia.

14. A man who claims to be deaf in the absence of any physical symptoms that would explain deafness probably has
    a. a social phobia.
    b. a conversion disorder.
    c. a dissiciative disorder.
    d. a specific phobia.

15. A woman who wandered away from her hometown and was discovered five years later in a distant cit and state using a different name and working in a different occupation experienced
    a. multiple personality disorder.
    b. depersonalization.
    c. dissociative amnesia.
    d. dissociative fugue.

16. A man who tells a therapist that he leaves his body and views himself and the situation he is in from a point ten feet in the air has
    a. a dissociative identity disorder.
    b. a generalized anxiety disorder.
    c. a depersonalization disorder.
    d. a specific phobia.

17. Sleeping difficulties, fatigue, significant weight loss, and feelings of worthlessness are characteristic of
    a. depression.
    b. schizophrenia.
    c. bipolar disorder.
    d. dissociative identity disorder.

18. The most serious complication of severe depression is
    a. comorbidity.
    b. the possibility of suicide.
    c. increased risk of heart attack.
    d. increased risk of substance abuse.

19. A typically quiet young woman has become very boisterous and wildly flirtatious, sleeping four hours a night but reporting boundless energy and that she has discovered a cure for cancer in her freshman biology lab. These symptoms are consistent with
    a. schizophrenia.
    b. psychosis.
    c. depression.
    d. mania.

20. The concordance rate is
    a. a measure of treatment efficacy for mental disorders.
    b. the percentage of twin pairs in which both twins have a disorder.
    c. an index of the proportion of the population that has a given disorder.
    d. the ratio of the incidence to the prevalence of a psychological disorder.

21. A recent college graduate who has been unable to find a job after six months of intense effort decides that he is unemployable and stops his job search. The man's behavior is an example of
    a. learned helplessness.
    b. arbitrary inference.
    c. a delusion.
    d. a specific phobia.

22. A college student who fails the first two tests she takes in an introductory psychology course decides that her lifelong goal of becoming a clinical psychologist is unrealistic and changes her major. The woman's behavior is an example of
    a. learned helplessness.
    b. arbitrary inference.
    c. a delusion.
    d. a specific phobia.

23. Schizophrenia is considered a psychotic disorder because
    a. a primary symptom is that a person loses contact with reality.
    b. it is treated most effectively with psychotherapy instead of drug therapy.
    c. inevitably results in institutionalization for the duration of a person's life.
    d. is a violent disorder requiring that many people with schizophrenia be incarcerated.

24. A 19-year-old college student has been having memory problems and incoherent thoughts, and he reports that he occasionally hears voices telling him what to do. These symptoms and his age suggest that he may be developing
    a. antisocial personality disorder.
    b. agoraphobia.
    c. schizophrenia.
    d. major depression.

25. The belief of a person diagnosed with schizophrenia that other people are "out to get him" is an example of
    a. a hallucination.
    b. a delusion.
    c. a specific phobia.
    d. a social phobia.

26. A person diagnosed with schizophrenia who hears voices telling her to act in unusual ways is experiencing
    a. hallucinations.
    b. delusions.
    c. fugue states.
    d. multiple personalities.

27. The subtype of schizophrenia characterized by unusual motor symptoms ranging from rigidity to hyperactivity is
    a. catatonic.
    b. disorganized.
    c. paranoid.
    d. residual.

28. The subtype of schizophrenia characterized by delusions of persecution or grandeur with auditory hallucinations is
    a. catatonic.
    b. disorganized.
    c. paranoid.
    d. residual.

29. The diagnosis for a con man who defrauds others without remorse is
    a. histrionic personality.
    b. dependent personality.
    c. schizotypal personality.
    d. antisocial personality.

30. The diagnosis for a person who is sexually aroused by some object of clothing is
    a. transsexualism.
    b. autopedophilia.
    c. voyeurism.
    d. fetishism.

Completion Items

Complete the following statements with key terms or concepts from the textbook.

1. The term used to describe behaviors that adversely affect a person's day-to-day living is _____.

2. The view that mental disorders have underlying organic causes is the _____ model.

3. The view that emphasizes the importance of society and culture in causing psychological disorders is the _____ model.

179

4. The number or percentage of people who ever had a particular disorder during a specified time period is _____.

5. The number or percentage of newly diagnosed cases of a particular disorder in a given population is _____.

6. A person who has a general feeling of apprehension with accompanying behavioral, cognitive, or physiological symptoms is experiencing _____.

7. A person who avoids public places or situations in which escape would be difficult would be given a diagnosis of _____.

8. A woman who has frequent flashbacks about a sexual assault and avoids ordinary social interactions with men is experiencing _____ disorder.

9. After a very stressful period at work, ending when he lost his job, a man suddenly who was unable to remember any details about the period was experiencing _____.

10. The diagnosis for a person who has three personalities is _____ disorder.

11. The mood disorder characterized by alternating episodes of mania and depression is _____ disorder.

12. Personality disorders are typically first observed during the developmental period of _____.

13. A student who is very dramatic and seductive, who needs constant reassurance that she is attractive, and whose moods change rapidly is said to have a _____ personality disorder.

14. A student who is very self-absorbed, who expects special treatment and adulation, and who envies any attention others receive is said to have a _____ personality disorder.

15. A student who is preoccupied with rules and details, who is a perfectionist but is indecisive, and who is unable to express affection is said to have a _____ personality disorder.

16. The diagnosis that would be made when a person believes he or she was born with the wrong sex organs is _____ disorder, or 17. _____.

18. Sexual arousal by objects or situations not considered sexual by most people is called _____.

19. A man arrested for indecent exposure is demonstrating the paraphilia called _____.

20. When in doubt about the classification of a psychological disorder or a particular set of symptoms, a therapist can consult the _____.

Critical Thinking Exercise

1. Why would childhood depression pose diagnostic problems different from those for adults?

Chapter Test Answers
Multiple Choice Items

1.b	11. a	21. a
2. b	12. c	22. b
3. d	13. c	23. a
4. a	14. b	24. c
5. c	15. d	25. b
6. b	16. c	26. a
7. d	17. a	27. a
8. a	18. b	28. c
9. b	19. d	29. d
10. d	20. b	30. d

Completion Items

1. dysfunctional	11. bipolar
2. medical	12. adolescence
3. sociocultural	13. histrionic
4. prevalence	14. narcissistic
5. incidence	15. obsessive-compulsive
6. anxiety	16. gender identity
7. agoraphobia	17. transsexualism
8. posttraumatic stress	18. paraphilia
9. dissociative amnesia	19. exhibitionism
10. dissociative identity	20. *DSM-IV-TR*

Critical Thinking Exercise

The depression rate among preschoolers is about 1%, among school-aged children it is 2% and it jumps to between 5% and 8% in adolescents. Diagnosing depression in young and very young children can be problematic because often they do not have the language to express what they are feeling. There is also some evidence to suggest that the symptoms common in adult depression, like appetite loss and difficulty sleeping, are less common in children. In addition, many people do not think that children are susceptible to depression because people tend to think of childhood as a time of low stress and relative happiness. The symptoms of depression may also change with age. For example, adolescents may appear angry rather than sad. Children are certainly aware of external stressors like family conflict, but they may express their inner discomfort and turmoil through somatic symptoms like stomach aches or headaches and irritability.

Key Vocabulary Terms: The terms listed in the margins of pages and entered in **boldface** type in the textbook are listed below with space for you to write the definitions. Remember that you may also want to create a list of the terms entered in italics in the textbook, especially those your instructor mentions in lectures. Again, you should try to write definitions *in your own words* because translating the terms into familiar language will facilitate retention.

dysfunctional

abnormal

insanity

medical model

psychodynamic model

behavioral model

cognitive model

sociocultural model

diagnosis

prevalence

incidence

anxiety

phobia

agoraphobia

social phobia

specific phobia

panic disorder

generalized anxiety disorder (GAD)

obsessive-compulsive disorder

posttraumatic stress disorder (PTSD)

somatoform disorders

hypochondriasis

somatization disorder

conversion disorder

dissociative disorders

dissociative amnesia

dissociative fugue

dissociative identity disorder (multiple personality)

depersonalization disorder

depression

mania

bipolar disorder

concordance rate

learned helplessness

arbitrary inference

schizophrenia

psychosis

delusion

hallucinations

personality disorders

antisocial personality disorder

gender identity disorder (transsexualism)

paraphilia

fetishism

CHAPTER 13

Therapy

THERAPY THROUGH THE AGES
The History of Therapy
Therapy and Therapists

PSYCHOLOGICALLY BASED THERAPIES
Psychoanalytic Therapy
Humanistic Therapies
Cognitive Therapies
Behavior Therapies
Cognitive Behavior Therapy
Group Therapies
Self-Help

THE EFFECTIVENESS OF PSYCHOTHERAPY
Psychotherapy and the Needs of Diversity
When to Begin Psychotherapy and What to Expect

BIOMEDICAL THERAPIES
Pharmacotherapy
Electroconvulsive Therapy
Psychosurgery

Notes from Class and the Textbook
Use the space provided in this outline to record notes from the textbook as well as from class lectures and discussion.

I. Therapy Through the Ages

    A. The History of Therapy

        1. Asylums and Hospitals

        2. Moral Therapy

        3. State Mental Hospitals

        4. New Forms of Treatment

        5. Deinstitutionalization

        6. The Community Mental Health Movement

Consider the *Study Tip* on p. 530 in the textbook.

    B. Therapy and Therapists

        1. Types of Therapists

        2. Stages of Therapy

II. Psychologically Based Therapies

    A. Psychoanalytic Therapy

        1. Free Association

        2. Dream Interpretation

        3. Resistance

        4. Transference

        5. Evaluation of Psychoanalysis

    B. Humanistic Therapies

        1. Client-Centered Therapy

    C. Cognitive Therapies

        1. Rational-Emotive Behavior Therapy

        2. Beck's Cognitive Therapy

Consider the *Psychological Detective* activity on p. 539 in the textbook.

Complete the *Hands On* activity on pp. 540-541 in the textbook.

Consider the *Study Tip* on p. 541 in the textbook.

    D. Behavior Therapies

        1. Systematic Desensitization

Consider the *Psychological Detective* activity on p. 542 in the textbook.

        2. Aversion Therapy

        3. Modeling

        4. Extinction

Consider the *Psychological Detective* activity on p. 544 in the textbook.

5. Punishment

6. Token Economy

Consider the *Psychological Detective* activity on p. 545 in the textbook.

E. Cognitive Behavior Therapy

Consider the *Psychological Detective* activity on p. 546 in the textbook.

F. Group Therapies

1. Marital and Family Therapy

G. Self-Help

III. The Effectiveness of Psychotherapy

A. Psychotherapy and the Needs of Diversity

B. When to Begin Psychotherapy and What to Expect

IV. Biomedical Therapies

A. Pharmacotherapy

    1. Antianxiety Drugs

    2. Antidepressant Drugs

    3. Mood Stabilizers

    4. Antipsychotic Drugs

Consider the *Study Tip* on p. 559 in the textbook.

    5. Variations in Drug Response Related to Ethnicity and Sex

    6. Pharmacotherapy: Summary and Evaluation

B. Electroconvulsive Therapy

Consider the *Psychological Detective* activity on p. 563 in the textbook.

Complete the *Myth or Science* activity on p. 563 in the textbook.

C. Psychosurgery

Chapter Test

In addition to completing the practice items that follow, remember to complete the items in the *Check Your Progress* sections in each chapter of the textbook. The answers to the **Multiple Choice Items**, **Completion Items**, and **Critical Thinking Exercises** are presented at the end of the **Chapter Test**.

Multiple Choice Items

Circle the letter that corresponds to the **best** alternative for each of the following items.

1. The term *bedlam* as a synonym for disorganized, unorganized conditions derives from
   a. the Greek word for chaos.
   b. a contraction of Bethlehem, which was part of the name of a London hospital.
   c. the first letters in each ancient, pre-Hippocrates form of psychological treatment.
   d. psychotherapeutic drugs were first administered to patients in the 1950's.

2. Philippe Pinel, Jean-Baptiste Pussin, and Benjamin Rush can be linked by the fact that they each
   a. recovered from mental illness.
   b. followed the mental health movement started by Dorothea Dix.
   c. advocated moral/humane treatment of mental patients.
   d. believed that psychological disorders were caused by demon possession.

3. A person taking an antianxiety drug is undergoing
   a. biomedical therapy.
   b. client-centered therapy.
   c. deinstitutionalization.
   d. rational-emotive behavior therapy.

4. A client undergoing psychological therapy would
   a. take an antidepressant drug.
   b. undergo electroconvulsive therapy.
   c. undergo psychosurgery.
   d. participate in systematic desensitization exercises.

5. After the initial introduction, the next stage of the therapy process is typically
   a. goal-setting.
   b. intervention.
   c. evaluation.
   d. follow-up.

6. The goal of psychoanalytic therapy is to
   a. modify unrealistic beliefs.
   b. uncover unconscious conflicts.
   c. modify maladaptive behaviors.
   d. develop a realistic sense of self.

7. A client who is being encouraged to say whatever comes to mind, no matter how unrelated to the client's perceived problem is
   a. resistance.
   b. transference.
   c. free association.
   d. catharsis.

8. A client who often interrupts psychoanalytic therapy sessions with discussions of specific topics that interrupt the flow of thoughts while free associating is demonstrating
   a. resistance.
   b. transference.
   c. free association.
   d. catharsis.

9. A woman in psychoanalytic therapy because she is unhappy with the attention her husband gives her attempts to initiate a relationship with her male therapist who gives her his undivided attention. The woman's behavior is an example of
   a. resistance.
   b. transference.
   c. free association.
   d. catharsis.

10. A humanistic therapy session would emphasize the client's
    a. unconscious motivations.
    b. prior experience with reinforcement.
    c. response to noxious stimuli.
    d. ability to solve their own problems.

11. The type of therapy designed to establish an environment in which a person finds solutions to his or her problems is
    a. aversion therapy.
    b. client-centered therapy.
    c. cognitive behavior therapy.
    d. psychoanalytic therapy.

12. A therapist's attitude of respect for a client as a person of worth is
    a. empathy.
    b. genuineness.
    c. unconditional positive regard.
    d. nondirectiveness.

13. Therapies designed to change a client's self-defeating thoughts are known as
    a. aversion therapies.
    b. client-centered therapies.
    c. cognitive therapies.
    d. psychoanalytic therapies.

14. A therapy session in which the therapist tells the client that his thoughts are irrational is typical of
    a. rational-emotive behavior therapy.
    b. aversion therapy.
    c. client-centered therapy.
    d. psychoanalytic therapy.

15. A therapist who is using systematic desensitization to help a client overcome a phobia of spiders is
    a. having the client read a number of books and articles about spiders.
    b. attempting to use principles of classical conditioning to extinguish the phobia.
    c. focusing on the source of the client's unconscious motivation to avoid spiders.
    d. working to convince the client of the unreasonable nature of the phobia.

16. The use of a drug called Antabuse that induces nausea when taken in combination with alcohol to help alcoholics stop drinking is an example of
    a. aversion therapy.
    b. cognitive therapy.
    c. cognitive behavior therapy.
    d. systematic desensitization.

17. After a brief vacation with his grandmother, a 3-year-old child is unwilling to sleep alone in his own room. The parents ignore the child's crying after putting her to bed and find that the length of time that she cries is shorter every night. This technique is called
    a. aversion therapy.
    b. stress inoculation.
    c. token economy.
    d. extinction.

18. A teacher who rewards students with stickers that can be exchanged for privileges or items like colored pencils
    a. has implemented unconditional positive regard.
    b. is practicing group therapy.
    c. is applying systematic desensitization.
    d. has established a token economy.

19. The feature of group therapy by which group members learn that others experience similar, equally serious problems, is
    a. self-disclosure.
    b. vicarious learning.
    c. norm clarification.
    d. social learning.

20. The feature of group therapy by which group members learn about themselves through observation of the therapist and other group members, is
    a. self-disclosure.
    b. vicarious learning.
    c. norm clarification.
    d. social learning.

21. The drug that would be prescribed to treat anxiety is
    a. Valium.
    b. Prozac.
    c. lithium.
    d. chlorpromazine.

22. The drug that would be prescribed to treat manic episodes in bipolar disorder is
    a. Valium.
    b. Prozac.
    c. lithium.
    d. chlorpromazine.

23. The drug that would be prescribed to treat schizophrenia is
    a. Valium.
    b. Prozac.
    c. lithium.
    d. chlorpromazine.

24. The serious side effect of antipsychotic drugs involving involuntary motor symptoms is
    a. restlessness.
    b. tardive dyskinesia.
    c. dizziness.
    d. grand mal seizures.

25. Electroconvulsive is used to treat severe
    a. mania.
    b. anxiety.
    c. sociopathy.
    d. depression.

Completion Items

Complete the following statements with key terms or concepts from the textbook.

1. The policy of discharging mentally ill patients from institutions so that they can be cared for in their home communities is _____.

2. Electroconvulsive therapy is an example of a _____ therapy.

3. The special relationship between a distressed person and a trained therapist is _____.

4. The largest group of mental health professionals is comprised of _____.

5. The content of a dream that a person remembers upon waking is the _____ content.
6. Client-centered therapy is also known as _____ therapy.

7. An effective method of behavior therapy based on observational learning is also known as _____.

8. Alcoholics Anonymous is an example of a _____.

9. The drugs used to treat bipolar disorder belong to the general group of _____.

10. A prefrontal lobotomy is a type of _____.

Critical Thinking Exercises
There no Critical Thinking Exercises for this chapter.

Chapter Test Answers
Multiple Choice Items

1. b	6. b	11. b	16. a	21. a
2. c	7. c	12. c	17. d	22. c
3. a	8. a	13. c	18. d	23. d
4. d	9. b	14. a	19. c	24. b
5. a	10. d	15. b	20. b	25. d

Completion Items

1. deinstitutionalization	6. nondirective
2. biomedical	7. modeling
3. psychotherapy	8. self-help group
4. social workers	9. mood stabilizers
5. manifest	10. psychosurgery

Key Vocabulary Terms: The terms listed in the margins of pages and entered in **boldface** type in the textbook are listed below with space for you to write the definitions. Remember that you may also want to create a list of the terms entered in italics in the textbook, especially those your instructor mentions in lectures. Again, you should try to write definitions *in your own words* because translating the terms into familiar language will facilitate retention.

deinstitutionalization

biomedical therapies

psychological therapies

psychotherapy

psychoanalytic therapy

free association

resistance

transference

humanistic therapies

client-centered therapy

cognitive therapies

rational-emotive behavior therapy

systematic desensitization

aversion therapy

token economy

cognitive behavior therapy (CBT)

group therapy

antianxiety drugs

antipsychotic drugs

tardive dyskinesia

electroconvulsive therapy (ECT)

psychosurgery

CHAPTER 14

Health Psychology

Notes from Class and the Textbook

Use the space provided in this outline to record notes from the textbook as well as from class lectures and discussion.

I. Health Psychology: An Overview

II. Stress and Illness

    A. The General Adaptation Syndrome

        1. Alarm Stage

        2. Resistance Stage

Complete the *Myth or Science* activity on p. 569 in the textbook.

        3. Exhaustion Stage

Consider the *Study Tip* on p. 570 in the textbook.

    B. Sources of Stress

        1. Catastrophes

        2. Major Life Events

Consider the *Psychological Detective* activity on p. 571 in the textbook.

        3. Acculturative Stress

        4. Posttraumatic Stress Disorder

        5. Everyday Hassles

    C. What Makes Events Stressful?

    D. How Stress and Disease May Be Related

        1. Psychoneuroimmunology

III. Lifestyle Influences on Disease Risk

    A. Smoking

        1. Who Smokes and Why?

        2. Quitting the Smoking Habit

    B. Heart Disease

        1. The Toxic Component of Type A Behavior

Complete the *Hands On* activity on pp. 580-581 in the textbook.

        2. Reducing the Risk of Heart Disease

    C. Environmental Factors

    D. Acquired Immunodeficiency Syndrome (AIDS)

        1. HIV: A Global Perspective

Consider the *Study Tip* on p. 581 in the textbook.

    E. Stress in the Workplace

        1. Burnout

        2. Stress and Women in the Workplace

Consider the *Psychological Detective* activity on p. 585 in the textbook.

IV. Coping with Stress

A. Psychological Moderators of Stress

      1. Explanatory Style

      2. Distraction

      3. Social Support

      4. Sense of Humor

      5. Religion and Spirituality

Consider the *Study Tip* on p. 588 in the textbook.

B. Reducing Arousal with Relaxation and Physical Activity

      1. Relaxation Techniques

      2. Physical Activity

      3. Does Physical Activity Reduce Stress?

Complete the *Myth or Science* activity on p. 591 in the textbook.

Consider the *Study Tip* on p. 591 in the textbook.

C. Resilience and Positive Psychology

Chapter Test

In addition to completing the practice items that follow, remember to complete the items in the *Check Your Progress* sections in each chapter of the textbook. The answers to the **Multiple Choice Items**, **Completion Items**, and **Critical Thinking Exercises** are presented at the end of the **Chapter Test**.

Multiple Choice Items

Circle the letter that corresponds to the ***best*** alternative for each of the following items.

1. A person who consulted a health psychologist to learn ways to improve his or her general health would receive recommendations to
   a. skip breakfast to lose weight.
   b. reduce the time spent sleeping to have more time to complete tasks that would otherwise increase stress.
   c. use seatbelts whenever riding in a vehicle.
   d. engage in 10 minutes of physical activity daily.

2. The stage of the general adaptation syndrome during which the fight-or-flight response occurs is the
   a. alarm stage.
   b. resistance stage.
   c. exhaustion stage.
   d. primitive fear stage.

3. During the resistance stage of the general adaptation syndrome, an organism
   a. prepares to fight.
   b. maintains a moderate level of arousal.
   c. experiences high heart rate and blood pressure.
   d. looks for ways to escape the stressful situation.

4. When demands for adjustment exceed the body's ability to respond, the body
   a. begins to develop resilience.
   b. experiences the posttraumatic syndrome.
   c. enters the exhaustion stage of the GAS.
   d. prepares again to fight or flee.

5. The term describing the stress a recent college graduate who has taken a job in a foreign country might experience is
   a. posttraumatic stress disorder.
   b. burnout.
   c. coping stress.
   d. acculturative stress.

6. An emergency medical technician who is having flashbacks and feeling anxious and guilty following several days spent helping victims of a natural disaster is experiencing
   a. the alarm stage.
   b. burnout.
   c. posttraumatic stress disorder.
   d. psychophysiological fear

7. Traffic jams, long lines in stores, and lost keys are examples of
   a. hassles.
   b. annoying habits.
   c. newsworthy events.
   d. symptoms of stress.

8. A person determining whether an approaching person in a dark parking lot is a threat is
   a. in the implementation stage.
   b. in the evaluation stage.
   c. making a primary appraisal.
   d. making a secondary appraisal.

9. Having decided that an approaching person in a dark parking lot is a threat and deciding to return to a lighted area means that a person has
   a. entered the implementation stage.
   b. entered the evaluation stage.
   c. made a primary appraisal.
   d. made a secondary appraisal.

10. Substances that trigger an immune response are
   a. endorphins.
   b. antigens.
   c. beta blockers.
   d. sera.

11. A psychologist investigating the influence of physiological and psychological factors on the immune system is interested in
   a. psychoneuroimmunology.
   b. longitudinal epidemiology.
   c. pandemics.
   d. rehabilitative counseling.

12. The percentage of smokers who smoked their first cigarette before the age of 18 is
   a. 25%.
   b. 50%.
   c. 75%.
   d. 90%.

13. A legitimate expectation for people who want to quit smoking is
   a. fewer bouts of insomnia.
   b. weight gain.
   c. lower anxiety.
   d. increased concentration.

14. The leading cause of death in the United States is
   a. heart disease.
   b. cancer following smoking.
   c. alcohol abuse.
   d. AIDS.

15. The person most likely to be at risk for heart disease
    a. has higher HDL than LDL.
    b. does not smoke.
    c. has female-type obesity.
    d. is physically active.

16. Characteristics of Type A behavior include
    a. a moderate need for achievement.
    b. the capacity to relax.
    c. competitiveness and aggressiveness.
    d. a high level of tolerance.

17. A person receiving a diagnosis of AIDS in the United States would most likely be
    a. 20 years old or younger.
    b. male.
    c. a member of a minority group.
    d. 50 years old or older.

18. A nurse who has been experiencing depressive symptoms, physical exhaustion, and problems at work is likely to be experiencing
    a. burnout.
    b. posttraumatic stress disorder.
    c. Type A behavior.
    d. resilience.

19. After completing a major term paper that generated a lot of stress, a student who decides to visit a friend at another college to relax is
    a. demonstrating resilience.
    b. using a coping strategy.
    c. reacting to burnout.
    d. trying progressive relaxation.

20. A person's capacity to rebound psychologically after confronting a stressful period is
    a. relaxation.
    b. biofeedback.
    c. coping.
    d. resilience.

Completion Items

Complete the following statements with key terms or concepts from the textbook.

1. Anything that causes a person to adjust and display the nonspecific stress response is a _____.

2. When a stressful situation continues beyond the alarm stage, the body progresses to the second stage of the general adaptation syndrome, which is known as the _____ stage.

3. When a student transfers to a different school, a teacher might expect the child to experience some degree of _____.

4. The body is protected from bacteria and viruses by the _____.

5. AIDS is caused by the _____.

6. A student who discusses a stressful major life event with a group of friends is seeking _____.

7. People who learn to breathe deeply, exhale slowly, and then relax various muscle groups are practicing _____.

8. The relaxation technique that involves the use of a mental device is the _____.

9. A person learning to use information from an electromyograph to control muscular tension is using _____.

10. The movement in psychology that emphasizes healthy psychological functioning is called _____.

Critical Thinking Exercise

Many researchers think that it is possible to condition the immune system to resist illness. However, the factors that enhance immune system functioning still need to be identified. A health psychologist is designing a study to investigate the effects of a placebo on improving immune system functioning. The hypothesis is that if a medication administered in the past has resulted in improved immune system functioning, then a person will believe that if the medicine is administered again, the immune system will function well a second time. The psychologist will test this hypothesis by creating two groups of participants. One group will receive a pill with the actual medicine, and the other group will receive a pill that contains no active ingredients (the placebo). Participants will be followed for 6 months to measure overall health.

1. What are the independent and dependent variables for this hypothetical study?

2. Given this basic experimental design, what are some of the extraneous variables that will need to be considered?

3. If the results show no significant difference between the two groups, what conclusions can reasonably be drawn?

Chapter Test Answers
Multiple Choice Items

1. c	6. c	11. a	16. c
2. a	7. a	12. d	17. c
3. b	8. c	13. b	18. a
4. c	9. d	14. a	19. b
5. d	10. b	15. a	20. d

Completion Items

1. stressor	6. social support
2. resistance	7. progressive relaxation
3. acculturative stress	8. relaxation response
4. immune system	9. biofeedback
5. human immunodeficiency virus	10. positive psychology

Critical Thinking Exercise

1. The independent variable is exposure to the medicine or the placebo. The dependent variable is the overall health (absence of illness) over 6 months.
2. One possible extraneous variable is the participant's previous experiences with medications. In general, everyone should have experienced successful results when using medications in the past. Another important consideration is that participants in the placebo group believe they are taking the real medication and are not aware of the placebo. The age of the participants and their overall health of the participants prior to starting the study are also possible extraneous variables.

3. If both groups are similarly healthy and experience no illness, the psychologist could conclude that immune enhancement can be improved just by taking a pill without medicine. However, the psychologist would not be able to conclude that the placebo effects could have a long-term impact on overall health. The next step could be to develop a second study to determine whether the behavior of taking medicine is conditioning an immune system response, and whether this conditioning can be maintained long-term. Such research would require a series of experiments and a longitudinal design.

Key Vocabulary Terms: The terms listed in the margins of pages and entered in **boldface** type in the textbook are listed below with space for you to write the definitions. Remember that you may also want to create a list of the terms entered in italics in the textbook, especially those your instructor mentions in lectures. Again, you should try to write definitions *in your own words* because translating the terms into familiar language will facilitate retention.

health psychology

stress

stressor

general adaptation syndrome (GAS)

acculturative stress

posttraumatic stress disorder (PTSD)

primary appraisal

secondary appraisal

immune system

antigens

Type A behavior

human immunodeficiency virus (HIV)

acquired immunodeficiency syndrome

burnout

coping

social support

progressive relaxation

relaxation response

biofeedback

resilience

positive psychology

CHAPTER 15

Social Psychology: The Individual in Society

Notes from Class and the Textbook
Use the space provided in this outline to record notes from the textbook as well as from class lectures and discussion.

I. Social Psychology and Culture

II. Social Cognition

    A. Impression Formation

        1. Aspects of the Perceiver

Consider the *Psychological Detective* activity on p. 597 of the textbook.

        2. Aspects of the Actor

        3. Appearance

        4. Speech

        5. Nonverbal Communication

Complete the *Hands On* activity on pp. 598-599 of the textbook.

        6. Prior Information

B. Social Judgments: Attributing Causes to Behavior

    1. Internal versus External Causes

Consider the *Psychological Detective* activity on p. 600 of the textbook.

    2. Distinctiveness

    3. Consistency

    4. Consensus

    5. Attributional Biases

Complete the *Myth or Science* activity on pp. 600-601 of the textbook.

    6. The Fundamental Attribution Error

Consider the *Psychological Detective* activity on p. 601 of the textbook

    7. The Actor-Perceiver Bias

Consider the *Study Tip* on p. 601 of the textbook

        8. Self-Serving Bias

Consider the *Psychological Detective* activity on p. 602 of the textbook

    C. Self-Perception

III. Attitudes

    A. Components of Attitudes: Affect, Cognition, and Behavior

    B. Functions of Attitudes

Consider the *Study Tip* on p. 603 of the textbook

    C. Measuring Attitudes

        1. Likert Scales

2. Behavioral Measures

C. How Are Attitudes Formed?

    1. Learning

    2. Cognitive Dissonance

IV. Interpersonal Relations

A. Attraction

    1. Proximity

    2. Affect and Emotions

    3. Reinforcement

    4. Similarity

B. Friendship

    1. Self-Disclosure

C. Love

    1. Sex Roles

2. Marital Satisfaction and Dissatisfaction

Consider the *Psychological Detective* activity on p. 610 of the textbook

   D. Prosocial Behavior: Helping Others

       1. Situational and Personal Influences on Helping Behavior

   E. Aggression

       1. Biological Views of Aggression

       2. Environmental Conditions and Aggression

Consider the *Psychological Detective* activity on p. 614 of the textbook

       3. International Terrorism

       4. Workplace Violence

       5. Sexual Aggression

V. Social Influences on Behavior

A. Persuasion

    1. Source Factors

    2. Expertise

    3. Attractiveness

Consider the *Psychological Detective* activity on p. 620 of the textbook

    4. Trustworthiness

    5. Message Factors

        a. Attention

    6. Drawing Conclusions

    7. Message Acceptance

Consider the *Psychological Detective* activity on p. 622 of the textbook

8. Primacy and Recency Effects

9. Channel Factors

Consider the *Psychological Detective* activity on p. 623 of the textbook

10. Audience Factors

11. What We Attend to: The Central and Peripheral Routes of Persuasion

Consider the *Study Tip* on p. 624 of the textbook

B. Obedience

C. Conformity and Compliance

VI. The Individual as Part of a Social Group

A. Social Facilitation

B. Social Loafing

C. Audiences and Coactors

    1. Deindividuation

D. Group Interactions and Group Decisions

    1. Group Formation and Effectiveness

    2. Brainstorming

Consider the *Psychological Detective* activity on p. 630 of the textbook

    3. Groupthink

E. Prejudice and Discrimination

    1. Prejudice

Consider the *Psychological Detective* activity on p. 632 of the textbook

    2. Discrimination

    3. Sources and Functions of Prejudice

4. Social Function

5. Emotional Function

6. How to Reduce Prejudice

Consider the *Study Tip* on p. 633 of the textbook

Chapter Test

In addition to completing the practice items that follow, remember to complete the items in the *Check Your Progress* sections in each chapter of the textbook. The answers to the **Multiple Choice Items**, **Completion Items**, and **Critical Thinking Exercises** are presented at the end of the **Chapter Test**.

Multiple Choice Items

Circle the letter that corresponds to the *best* alternative for each of the following items.

1. The belief that one's own country or culture is superior to all other countries or cultures is
   a. prejudice.
   b. collectivism.
   c. self-serving bias.
   d. ethnocentrism.

2. If four students assigned to complete a group project select a topic that each knows something about instead of the topic each would have selected on his or her own, the students are demonstrating
   a. self-disclosure.
   b. collectivism.
   c. interdependence theory.
   d. social facilitation.

3. A social psychologist whose research is about impression formation is interested in
   a. how people form opinions about others.
   b. how people present themselves.
   c. why people make the fundamental attribution error.
   d. why people resist forming impressions on their first exposure to others.

4. A stereotype is
   a. an individual's attempt to behave to match a group standard.
   b. a set of beliefs about members of a particular group.
   c. an individual's decision to share personal information.
   d. a bias toward members of one's in-group.

5. Although he had not planned to participate, a student selected to be hypnotized by a comedian-hypnotist at a local club is soon clucking like a chicken, playing the role of "the human plank", and being generally entertaining. the student's behavior is an example of
   a. self-disclosure.
   b. attribution theory.
   c. the self-fulfilling prophecy.
   d. the fundamental attribution error.

6. A social psychologist told half a psychology class that a guest lecturer was warm and approachable and the other half that the lecturer was cold and aloof. At the end of the lecture, the first group of students rated the lecture more favorably than the second group. This experiment demonstrates
   a. the effects of prior information.
   b. the self-serving bias.
   c. cognitive dissonance.
   d. the fundamental attribution error.

7. The tendency to make internal attributions when we are successful and external attributions when we fail is called the:
   a. self-serving bias.
   b. cognitive dissonance.
   c. unconscious motivation.
   d. fundamental attribution error.

8. A student torn between taking a part-time job and having more spending money and declining the job offer and continuing to make good grades is experiencing
   a. confusion.
   b. the self-fulfilling prophecy.
   c. a self-serving bias.
   d. cognitive dissonance.

9. The extent to which people seek out others who are similar and attempt to remain in close proximity to them defines
   a. conformity.
   b. companionate love.
   c. attraction.
   d. friendship.

10. Two students who are attracted to each other when they enroll at a university, and who establish a relationship governed by implicit rules
    a. are experiencing companionate love.
    b. have formed a friendship.
    c. are exhibiting a self-fulfilling prophecy.
    d. are exemplifying interdependence theory.

11. Two people in a relationship based on passionate love can expect
    a. a long-term relationship.
    b. a high level of commitment.
    c. strong emotional reactions.
    d. few differences if they are different cultures.

12. A student having doubts about remaining in a romantic relationship, and who is comparing the costs and rewards of remaining in the relationship is
    a. applying interdependence theory.
    b. risking a fundamental attribution error.
    c. considering how to make a self-disclosure.
    d. brainstorming.

13. A person who tutors children after school for the minimum wage is demonstrating
    a. reciprocity.
    b. compliance.
    c. obedience.
    d. prosocial behavior.

14. A person who joins a volunteer organization formed to teach illiterate people to read is exhibiting
    a. reciprocity.
    b. altruism.
    c. the just world belief.
    d. friendship.

15. The tendency for a members of a group of people to be less likely to provide assistance to a person in trouble than an individual is
    a. the bystander effect.
    b. conformity.
    c. disobedience.
    d. an example of the social identity theory.

16. A student who physically assaults his roommate because he believes his roommate has stolen from him is exhibiting
    a. frustration.
    b. instrumental aggression.
    c. hostile aggression.
    d. reactance.

17. A student who is injured while being pulled from a car by a carjacker is a victim of
    a. frustration.
    b. instrumental aggression.
    c. hostile aggression.
    d. reactance.

18. A source factor that would contribute to an attractive person's persuasiveness is
    a. expertise.
    b. conformity.
    c. compliance.
    d. reciprocity.

19. The fact that after a period of time a sales message from a person since convicted of fraud becomes more effective demonstrates
    a. reactance.
    b. self-serving bias.
    c. the fundamental attribution error.
    d. the sleeper effect.

20. Another term for what is popularly known as "reverse psychology" is
    a. reactance.
    b. self-serving bias.
    c. groupthink.
    d. hindsight bias.

21. Military personnel who respond to orders from superior officers are exhibiting
    a. conformity.
    b. reactance.
    c. obedience.
    d. altruism.

22. A student who stops wearing the same clothes he wore in high school after joining a college social organization is exhibiting
    a. conformity.
    b. reactance.
    c. obedience.
    d. altruism.

23. A generally honest, well-behaved student who is one of five students to be expelled from school because he agreed with the other students to purchase a term paper for a group project is a victim of
    a. the foot-in-the-door effect.
    b. the risky-shift phenomenon.
    c. social loafing.
    d. social facilitation.

24. The observation that group decision making enhances or amplifies the original opinions of the group's members is
    a. reciprocity.
    b. risk-taking.
    c. deindividuation.
    d. group polarization.

25. If a person is approached by a political candidate and consents to place a campaign sign in her yard, and later agrees to make a generous financial contribution to the candidate's campaign, the candidate is using the
    a. risky-shift phenomenon.
    b. foot-in-the-door effect.
    c. door-in-the-face technique.
    d. interdependence theory.

26. Children who read better aloud when they are reading to the class than when they are reading only to the teacher are demonstrating
  a. social conformity.
  b. social facilitation.
  c. social loafing.
  d. conformity.

27. An instructor who assigns a group project and does not include a method for evaluating each member's contribution to the final product is encouraging
  a. social conformity.
  b. social facilitation.
  c. social loafing.
  d. conformity.

28. A minority of students who are opposed to spending some of the money raised for charity on a dinner for people who collected the donations, but who vote in favor of the dinner to maintain group harmony are demonstrating
  a. deindividuation.
  b. brainstorming.
  c. reactance.
  d. groupthink.

29. An unjustified negative attitude toward an individual based on the individual's membership in a particular group is
  a. groupthink.
  b. prejudice.
  c. discrimination.
  d. deindividuation.

30. A student who is denied admission to a gathering sponsored by a social organization because he or she is a member of a different social organization is experiencing
  a. groupthink.
  b. prejudice.
  c. discrimination.
  d. deindividuation.

Completion Items

Complete the following statements with key terms or concepts from the textbook.

1. People who place their own goals above those of the group are exhibiting _____.

2. A set of beliefs about members of a particular group is known as _____.

3. The amount of personal information a person is willing to share with others is called _____.

4. A student who believes that another student received a higher grade because the second student is more intelligent when the second student actually had a copy of a test from the previous semester is demonstrating the _____.

5. The belief that good things happen to good people and bad things happen to bad people is a statement of the _____.

6. Evaluative judgments about people, objects, or thoughts are _____.

7. A questionnaire comprised of statements to which respondents respond on a scale ranging from "Strongly Disagree" to "Strongly Agree" is a _____.

8. The theory that stresses the costs and rewards involved in interpersonal relationships is _____ theory.

9. The general outcome expected from a particular relationship is the _____.

10. The long-lasting form of love involving commitment is _____ love.

11. Physical or psychological behavior performed with the intent of doing harm is _____.

12. The observation that a person becomes more aggressive when she is frustrated than when she is not frustrated supports the _____.

13. The use of social influence to cause people to change attitudes or behavior is _____.

14. A person who changes a behavior in response to indirect social pressures is _____.

15. If a person changes behavior in response to a request, as opposed to a command, the person is demonstrating _____.

16. If a person contributes $5 after refusing to donate $100, the solicitor has used the _____.
17. If a student helps her roommate with an assignment and then asks the roommate to help clean the apartment, the student is applying the concept of _____.

18. If a high school student who refuses to complete an assignment is joined by several classmates who also refuse to complete the assignment, the classmates are _____.

19. A couple who tried giving candy to trick-or-treaters on Halloween using the honor system were chagrined when they returned from a party to find that the candy and the bowls in which it was placed were gone. If the theft was performed by a group of trick-or-treaters, a possible explanation is _____.

20. The technique used by a business owner who conducted a meeting in which employees were asked to express any ideas they had to improve sales was _____.

Critical Thinking Exercise

A group of educated, married men has formed an organization designed to change their government's policies. No one knows about this organization except the men in the group. Many of these men have moderate incomes, but they believe they do not have a fair share of their country's economic wealth. They see people who have nicer cars, homes, and clothes. However, these men do not feel that they personally can do much about their lack of money. Instead, they blame their lack of money on government policy and the general unfairness of people in the country. Therefore, they have made plans to destroy government buildings and otherwise frighten the public in order to force the government to change its policies so they will have the same opportunities to increase their incomes that they believe other people have.

What social psychology terms and concepts are identifiable in the preceding scenario?

Chapter Test Answers
Multiple Choice Items

1. d	11. c	21. c
2. b	12. a	22. a
3. a	13. d	23. b
4. b	14. b	24. d
5. c	15. a	25. b
6. a	16. c	26.b
7. a	17. b	27. c
8. d	18. a	28. d
9. c	19. d	29. b
10. b	20. a	30. c

Completion Items

1. individualism	11. aggression
2. attribution	12. frustration-aggression hypothesis
3. self-disclosure	13. persuasion
4. fundamental attribution error	14. conformity
5. just world belief	15. compliance
6. attitudes	16. door-in-the-face technique
7. Likert scale	17. reciprocity
8. interdependence theory	18. coacters
9. comparison level	19. deindividuation
10. companionate	20. brainstorming

Critical Thinking Exercises

The group of men has perceived in-groups and out-groups. In contrast to the view presented in the textbook, these men would like to be in the out-group, i.e., be members of the wealthy group who have nice cars and homes. Based on their decision to destroy buildings and create terror in the public, they would be labeled terrorists. The frustration-aggression hypothesis would help to explain their decision to engage in aggression. The group is frustrated that they cannot have what others have, and they plan to displace that aggression onto the government. These men are also making external attributions to justify their perceived lack of money; the government is at fault.

Key Vocabulary Terms: The terms listed in the margins of pages and entered in **boldface** type in the textbook are listed below with space for you to write the definitions. Remember that you may also want to create a list of the terms entered in italics in the textbook, especially those your instructor mentions in lectures. Again, you should try to write definitions *in your own words* because translating the terms into familiar language will facilitate retention.

social psychology

ethnocentrism

individualism

collectivism

impression formation

attribution

stereotype

self-fulfilling prophecy

self-disclosure

fundamental attribution error

self-serving bias

just world belief

attitudes

Likert scale

cognitive dissonance

attraction

friendship

passionate love

compassionate love

interdependence theory

comparison level

prosocial behavior

altruism

bystander effect

aggression

hostile aggression

instrumental aggression

frustration-aggression hypothesis

persuasion

sleeper effect

reactance

obedience

conformity

risky-shift phenomenon

group polarization

compliance

foot-in-the-door effect

door-in-the-face technique

reciprocity

social facilitation

social loafing

coacters

deindividuation

brainstorming

groupthink

prejudice

discrimination

CHAPTER 16

Industrial, Organizational, and Other Applications of Psychology

Notes from Class and the Textbook
Use the space provided in this outline to record notes from the textbook as well as from class lectures and discussion.

I. The "I" and the "O" of Industrial/Organizational Psychology

    A. Industrial Psychology

        1. Job Analysis

        2. Predicting and Selecting

Consider the *Psychological Detective* activity on p. 640 in the textbook.

        3. Training

Consider the *Study Tip* on p. 642 in the textbook.

        4. Performance Appraisal

    B. Organizational Psychology

        1. Motivation

2. Job Satisfaction

Consider the *Study Tip* on p. 648 in the textbook.

II. Human-Factors Psychology

    A. Person-Machine System

    B. Workplace Design

        1. Safety

III. Other Applications of Psychology in the Real World

    A. Forensic Psychology

        1. Memory and the Law

        2. Insanity, Competence, and Civil Commitment

    B. Community and Environmental Psychology

        1. Community Psychology

        2. Environmental Psychology

C. Occupational Health Psychology

    1. Workplace Dangers

    2. Preventing Disease and Promoting Good Health in the Workplace

D. Sport Psychology

    1. Enhancing Athletic Performance

    2. Coaching

    3. Fan Violence

Consider the *Study Tip* on p. 658 in the textbook.

Chapter Test

In addition to completing the practice items that follow, remember to complete the items in the *Check Your Progress* sections in each chapter of the textbook. The answers to the **Multiple Choice Items**, **Completion Items**, and **Critical Thinking Exercises** are presented at the end of the **Chapter Test**.

Multiple Choice Items

Circle the letter that corresponds to the *best* alternative for each of the following items.

1. An industrial psychologist conducting a job analysis who focuses on the tasks required by the job is taking a
    a.   job-oriented approach.
    b.   safety-oriented approach.
    c.   worker-oriented approach.
    d.   human-environmental approach.

2. An industrial psychologist conducting a job analysis who focuses on the human factors associated with the job is taking a
    a. job-oriented approach.
    b. safety-oriented approach.
    c. worker-oriented approach.
    d. human-environmental approach.

3. An industrial psychologist advising a company on their selection process would recommend
    a. asking questions about lifestyle instead of questions based on job analysis.
    b. using a single interview with the same interviewer for all applicants.
    c. tailoring questions for each applicant based on the applicant's personal background.
    d. conducting multiple interviews, each with a different interviewer.

4. A psychologist hired by a restaurant chain to improve the performance of managers of individual restaurants in the chain will be
    a. concerned about ergonomics.
    b. involved in training.
    c. most likely an occupational health psychologist.
    d. modifying the work environment.

5. The training method in which a trainee mimics the behavior of experienced employees is
    a. simulation.
    b. job rotation.
    c. vestibule training.
    d. on-the-job training.

6. The training method in which a trainee works on a smaller version of a production line so that the main production activity is unaffected is
    a. simulation.
    b. job rotation.
    c. vestibule training.
    d. on-the-job training.

7. After six months on the job, an employee whose work has just been rated on a number of criteria by her supervisor is undergoing
    a. training.
    b. applicant screening.
    c. a formal exit interview.
    d. performance evaluation.

8. The rating error committed when a person is rated favorably on all performance dimensions because the rate has a positive overall impression of the employee is the
    a. halo error.
    b. leniency error.
    c. attribution error.
    d. central tendency error.

9. If all the employees in a unit fail to receive a pay increase because the supervisor has ranked all of them in the middle of the evaluation scale, the supervisor has committed the
    a. halo effect.
    b. leniency error.
    c. attribution error.
    d. central tendency error.

10. A psychologist who studies labor unions examining the rules and benefits of membership and the social dynamics of members is
    a. a personnel psychologist.
    b. an industrial psychologist.
    c. an organizational psychologist.
    d. a human-factors psychologist.

11. The most widely investigated work attitude in organizational psychology is
    a. job satisfaction.
    b. employer loyalty.
    c. employee benefits appreciation.
    d. worker efficiency.

12. Following a serious wreck, the psychologist who could be employed to redesign the instrument panel used in high-speed trains so that engineers can stop the trains more quickly is
    a. an engineering psychologist.
    b. an ergonomic psychologist.
    c. a community psychologist.
    d. a human-factors psychologist.

13. A psychologist who has been hired to redesign a machine to prevent accidents attributable to the fact that many workers are not strong enough to operate the lever used to turn the machine off in emergency situations is
    a. an engineering psychologist.
    b. an ergonomic psychologist.
    c. a community psychologist.
    d. a human-factors psychologist.

14. The psychologist who might recommend that a worker who has suffered an injury that limits his ability to perform his previous job as it is structured be retrained instead of fired is
    a. an engineering psychologist.
    b. an ergonomic psychologist.
    c. a community psychologist.
    d. a human-factors psychologist.

15. The task a psychologist who works in the area of engineering anthropometry would be expected to perform is
    a. helping professional athletes overcome motivation problems.
    b. assessing work environments to remove health hazards.
    c. assisting attorneys as they prepare to defend clients with mental disorders.
    d. designing larger seats for airplanes owned by professional sports teams.

16. The task a forensic psychologist would be expected to perform is
    a. helping professional athletes overcome motivation problems.
    b. assessing work environments to remove health hazards.
    c. assisting attorneys as they prepare to defend clients with mental disorders.
    d. designing larger seats for airplanes owned by professional sports teams.

17. After a series of incidents involving several different social organizations, the type of psychologist a university president might hire to assess the relationship between university-sponsored social organizations and the university as a whole is
    a. an environmental psychologist.
    b. an ergonomic psychologist.
    c. a community psychologist.
    d. a human-factors psychologist.

18. A psychologist who has planned a study to compare the responses of students in a psychology classroom with the responses of a crowd at a concert in a mock emergency situation is
    a.   an environmental psychologist.
    b.   an ergonomic psychologist.
    c.   a community psychologist.
    d.   a human-factors psychologist.

19. The task an occupational psychologist would be expected to perform is
    a.   helping professional athletes overcome motivation problems.
    b.   assessing work environments to remove health hazards.
    c.   assisting attorneys as they prepare to defend clients with mental disorders.
    d.   designing larger seats for airplanes owned by professional sports teams.

20. The task a sports psychologist would be expected to perform is
    a.   helping professional athletes overcome motivation problems.
    b.   assessing work environments to remove health hazards.
    c.   assisting attorneys as they prepare to defend clients with mental disorders.
    d.   designing larger seats for airplanes owned by professional sports teams.

Completion Items

Complete the following statements with key terms or concepts from the textbook.

1. A thorough description of job responsibilities and the qualities and abilities of employees needed to perform them is a _____.

2. An interview in which all candidates answer the same questions is said to be _____.

3. The type of interview involving different questions for individual applicants used by many interviewers who believe they can "size people up" during an interview is said to be _____.

4. A group of employees learning to use an updated computer database are undergoing _____.

5. An employee whose performance appraisal is based on the dollar amount of sales is based on _____ criteria.

6. A performance appraisal in which supervisors must assign certain percentages of employees to categories from superior to poor is based on _____.

7. A supervisor who assigns better than average ratings to all employees is committing the _____.

8. A psychologist who suggests that the cutting surface in a restaurant be raised 10" is applying _____.

9. A psychologist who suggests that employees who operate a particular machine demonstrate the ability to lift 50 pounds with one hand is applying _____.

10. When occupational health psychologists work with employees to encourage positive attitudes about work safety, the psychologists are emphasizing the _____.

Critical Thinking Exercise

Sort the following activities into Industrial (I) or Organizational (O) categories:

Assessment of job satisfaction
Job analysis
Conducting performance evaluations
Assessing leadership effectiveness
Increasing profitability
Assessing quality of work life
Training
Setting performance standards
Selection & placement

Chapter Test Answers
Multiple Choice Items

1. a	6. c	11. a	16. c
2. c	7. d	12. d	17. c
3. d	8. a	13. b	18. a
4. b	9. d	14. a	19. b
5. d	10. c	15. d	20. a

Completion Items

1. job analysis	6. forced categories
2. structured	7. leniency error
3. unstructured	8. ergonomics
4. training	9. engineering psychology
5. objective or hard	10. safety climate

Critical Thinking Exercises

Assessment of job satisfaction - Organizational
Job analysis - Industrial
Conducting performance evaluations - Industrial
Assessing leadership effectiveness - Organizational
Increasing profitability - Organizational
Assessing quality of work life - Organizational
Training - Industrial
Setting performance standards - Industrial
Selection & placement - Industrial

Key Vocabulary Terms: The terms listed in the margins of pages and entered in **boldface** type in the textbook are listed below with space for you to write the definitions. Remember that you may also want to create a list of the terms entered in italics in the textbook, especially those your instructor mentions in lectures. Again, you should try to write definitions *in your own words* because translating the terms into familiar language will facilitate retention.

industrial and organizational (I/O) psychology

job analysis

training

performance evaluation

organizational psychology

human-factors psychology

ergonomics

engineering psychology

engineering anthropometry

forensic psychology

community psychology

environmental psychology

occupational health psychologist

safety climate

sport psychologist

NOTES